BOUNDARIES
IN DATING

Resources by Henry Cloud and John Townsend

Books

Boundaries (and workbook)
Boundaries in Dating (and workbook)
Boundaries in Marriage (and workbook)
Boundaries with Kids (and workbook)
Boundaries with Teens (Townsend)
Changes That Heal (and workbook) (Cloud)
Hiding from Love (Townsend)
How People Grow (and workbook)
How to Have That Difficult Conversation You've Been Avoiding
Making Small Groups Work
The Mom Factor (and workbook)
Raising Great Kids
Raising Great Kids Workbook for Parents of Preschoolers
Raising Great Kids Workbook for Parents of School-Age Children
Raising Great Kids Workbook for Parents of Teenagers
Safe People (and workbook)
12 "Christian" Beliefs That Can Drive You Crazy

Video Curriculum

Boundaries
Boundaries in Dating
Boundaries in Marriage
Boundaries with Kids
Raising Great Kids for Parents of Preschoolers
ReGroup (with Bill Donahue)

Audio

Boundaries
Boundaries in Dating
Boundaries in Marriage
Boundaries with Kids
Boundaries with Teens (Townsend)
Changes That Heal (Cloud)
How People Grow
How to Have That Difficult Conversation You've Been Avoiding
Making Small Groups Work
The Mom Factor
Raising Great Kids

BOUNDARIES IN DATING

HOW HEALTHY
CHOICES
GROW HEALTHY
RELATIONSHIPS

DR. HENRY CLOUD & DR. JOHN TOWNSEND

We want to hear from you. Please send your comments about this book to us in care of zreview@zondervan.com. Thank you.

ZONDERVAN

Boundaries in Dating
Copyright © 2000 by Henry Cloud and John Townsend

This title is also available as a Zondervan ebook. Visit www.zondervan.com/ebooks.

This title is also available in a Zondervan audio edition. Visit www.zondervan.fm.

Requests for information should be addressed to:

Zondervan, *Grand Rapids, Michigan 49530*

Library of Congress Cataloging-in-Publication Data

Cloud, Henry.
     Boundaries in dating : how healthy choices grow healthy relationships /
Henry Cloud and John Townsend.
          p.   cm.
     ISBN 978-0-310-20034-5 (softcover)
     1. Dating (Social customs). 2. Dating (Social customs)—Religious aspects—
Christianity. 3. Single people—Conduct of life. I. Townsend, John Sims, 1952-
II. Title.
HQ801. C59   2000
646.7′7—dc21   99-057936

The examples used in this book are compilations of stories from real situations. But names, facts, and issues have been altered to protect confidentiality while illustrating the points.

Published in association with Yates & Yates, www.yates2.com.

Printed in the United States of America

To Matilda Townsend (1902–1983),
who contributed greatly to my life
—J. T.

To singles everywhere, with the hope that your
dating experience can realize the desires of
your heart, and God's best for you
—H. C.

Contents

Part 4: Solving Dating Problems: When Your Date Is the Problem

Acknowledgments

*W*ith gratitude to our agent, Sealy Yates; our publisher, Scott Bolinder; and our editor, Sandra Vander Zicht. And thanks to our marketing director, John Topliff, whose thoughtful understanding of the needs of our readers makes publishing much more enjoyable.

I would like also to acknowledge Guy and Christi Owen, who were there for me through my long years of dating.

I would like to acknowledge Lillie Nye for her efforts to get this material to singles everywhere and her input along the way.

Thanks to the Daytona group for sharing your stories and courage.

Thanks to the *Christian Single* magazine staff, who have helped me to understand the current dynamics that singles face and who also provide a great resource to help them.

Thanks to Single Adult Ministries for inviting us over the years to share with you.

Thanks to Jim Burns, president of the National Institute of Youth Ministry, for his input regarding the dating plight of teens today and his spin of the current thinking in the church. Your ministry has changed the face of dating for literally millions worldwide. They are safer than if you had not been there over the years.

—H.C.

Thanks to Roy and Susan Zinn for your work with singles at the North Carolina State Navigators ministry. Your compassion and ministry have touched many, including myself.

Thanks to Mike Hoisington and Cary Tamura for colaboring with the Single Focus class at First Evangelical Free Church in Fullerton, California. Your initiative and leadership for singles has borne good fruit through the years. Thanks to Chuck Swindoll, senior pastor at that time, for giving us permission to think creatively about the struggles of singles.

Thanks to Scott Rae, former singles pastor at Mariners Church in Irvine, California. Your thoughtful efforts to help singles grow spiritually, and your many opportunities to have us speak to your groups, are much appreciated.

—J. T.

Why Dating?

A few years back I was doing a seminar for singles in the Midwest when the question came from the floor, "Dr. Cloud, what is the biblical position on dating?" At first, I thought I had misheard the question, so I asked the woman to repeat it. And the question came out the same as the first time.

"What do you mean, 'the biblical position'?" I asked.

"Well, do you think that dating is a biblical thing to do?" the woman explained.

Once I heard her question, I thought she was kidding, but I soon realized she was not. I had heard people ask about the biblical position on capital punishment or euthanasia, but never on dating.

"I do not think the Bible gives a 'position' on dating," I said. "Dating is an activity that people do, and as with a lot of other things, the Bible does not talk about it. What the Bible *does* talk about is being a loving, honest, growing person in whatever you do. So, I would have to say that the biblical position on dating has much more to do with the person you are and are becoming than whether or not you date. The biblical position on dating would be to date in a holy way.

"In fact, God grows people up through dating relationships in the same way that he grows them up in many other life activities. The question is not whether or not you are dating. The questions are more along the lines of 'Who are you in your dating and who are you becoming in your dating? What is the fruit of your dating for you and for the people that you date? How are you treating them? What are you learning?' And a host of other issues that the Bible is very clear about. It is mainly about your character growth and how you treat people."

"So, you think it is okay to date?" she pressed.

"Of course, I do, but it is only okay to date within biblical guidelines, which by the way are not burdensome. They will save your life and help you to make sure you end up with a good person to marry," I said, chuckling on the inside about how often Christians want a rule.

I thought this was the end of it until the same question kept coming up around the country whenever I would speak to singles. Over and over again, I was asked if dating were an okay thing to do or not. I was curious about why people were asking the same question.

So, one day, I asked where these questions were coming from. I was told that a movement was arising from a book called *I Kissed Dating Goodbye* by Joshua Harris. The premise of the book is that dating is not a good idea, and many people were giving it up. As I continued to investigate, the movement went even further than the book in some circles. Many Christians were saying that dating was sinful in and of itself; others were at least feeling as if people who were still dating were less spiritual than those who didn't. It was becoming the "Christian" thing to forego dating. I thought at first that this was just in some circles, but the more I traveled around I was hearing it all over the country.

So we read *I Kissed Dating Goodbye,* and in this chapter we will share some of our reactions. We strongly disagree with the idea that all people should give up dating for several reasons. But before we get into the specifics, we want to validate the reasons behind this movement.

No one would take such a stance against dating without good reason, and the reason people are giving up dating seems to be this: pain, disillusionment, and detrimental effects to their spiritual life. In other words, dating has not helped them to grow, find a mate, or become a more spiritual person. So, it makes sense to kiss it good-bye.

And we empathize with this pain. As we have seen over the years working with many singles and being single for a long time ourselves (both of us were well into our thirties before we married), dating can cause a lot of hurt and suffering. Many people become disillusioned in the process, and they feel like they do not know how to make it work. They experience heartbreak, they repeatedly pick the "wrong type," they can't find the "right type," or they find the "right type" and they don't like him or her as much as the wrong type. They have trouble integrating their spiritual life into dating. And they question what to do with physical attraction and moral limits, as well as wonder when to move from casual dating to a more significant relationship.

For many people the pain and suffering of dating becomes too much, and they are ready for an alternative. And out of this motivation, we concur with the followers of the no-dating movement and its proponents. The pain of dating is not worth it if it does not lead to anything good. We understand Mr. Harris's motive for writing this book.

But we disagree with his conclusion. While we agree that the hurt must stop, we don't think that dating is the problem. We think people are. In the same way that cars don't kill people, drunk drivers do, dating does not hurt people, but dating in out-of-control ways does. Paul's advice to the Colossians is sound: "Since you died with Christ to the basic principles of this world, why, as though you still belonged to it, do you submit to its rules: 'Do not handle! Do not taste! Do not touch!'? These are all destined to perish with use, because they are based on human commands and teachings. Such regulations indeed have an *appearance of wisdom*, with their self-imposed worship, their false humility and their harsh treatment of the body, *but they lack any value in restraining sensual indulgence"* (Colossians 2:20–23, italics ours). Paul cautioned the Colossians that making rules and abstaining from certain practices would never develop the maturity they needed to live life.

Human problems are matters of the heart, the soul, one's orientation toward God, and a whole host of other maturity issues. As Paul says, avoiding certain things you could engage in destructively does not cure your basic problem of immaturity, which is internal not external. You may be immature and not able to handle dating, so you abstain from dating. But, unless you do something to grow up, you will still be immature, and you will take that immaturity right into marriage.

Avoiding dating isn't the way to cure the problems encountered in dating. The cure is the same as the Bible's cure for all of life's problems, and that is *spiritual growth leading to maturity*. Learning how to love, follow God, be honest and responsible, treat others as you would want to be treated, develop self-control, and build a fulfilling life will ensure better dating.

Before we tell you in this book how to date well, we want to point out some reasons why we think you shouldn't kiss dating good-bye and some more reasons why we think dating can be great.

In his book in the chapter "The Seven Habits of Highly Defective Dating," Joshua Harris talks about the following "negative tendencies" of dating.

1. Dating leads to intimacy but not necessarily to commitment.
2. Dating tends to skip the "friendship" stage of a relationship.
3. Dating often mistakes a physical relationship for love.
4. Dating often isolates a couple from other vital relationships.

5. Dating, in many cases, distracts young adults from their primary responsibility of preparing for the future.
6. Dating can cause discontentment with God's gift of singleness.
7. Dating creates an artificial environment for evaluating another person's character.

All of these problem scenarios are created by people and the way that they date. Throughout the rest of this book we will address each one of these by looking at the lack of appropriate structure within, among other things, a person's character, support system, values, and relationship with God. In other words, a lack of *boundaries*.

Each one of these scenarios has to do with some aspects of character immaturity, such as fusion, dependency, or self-centeredness. A loss of boundaries occurs when an immature person gives up all of his or her structure, internal and external, and fuses with an ideal, a person, or something else to avoid maturing. The immature, idealized "falling in love" that we have all seen as destructive is always a problem in which someone needs to be brought back to reality. If someone has this tendency, they need character and spiritual growth to mature enough to face life and relationships in a more balanced way. And we think that God can provide that.

Throughout the book, we talk about all of these problems, and the boundaries that will cure them. God gives us principles to guide us in life. Because we can trust his ways, we are free to grow and develop a life as we mature. We do not have to avoid life, or maturity.

Harris builds his case on one example after another of selfish gratification of passion at the expense of another person, or of heartbreak, or of immature, dependent, addictive romance. None of those situations are caused by dating, but by the immaturity of the people involved. We all know many situations where more mature and godly teens, young adults, and older adults dated in very growth-producing and mature ways, and they are very grateful for the experience. Harris's logic seems to be:

Person A dated person B.
Person A or B or both got hurt.
Dating is bad.

This is a little like saying because there is divorce, no one should get married. Or because there are car accidents, no one should drive. Many singles date very responsibly, and they learn and grow through the experience. Both parties are the better for it, and they are more prepared for a later commitment.

Harris, however, is right about this: *some* people should not date, at least for a while. Just as some people should not drive, or should not ever drink, or should not do other things the Bible leaves as free territory, some people should not date. The biblical principle is that these people might have a weakness or immaturity that could cause them to stumble, and for this reason, refraining from a certain activity is best.

One internationally known youth worker I consulted confirmed this. He said, "Refraining from dating is probably a good idea for a small percent of the teenagers we work with. The rest need to be dating and learning how to handle all that dating brings up in the maturity cycle." This is what we think as well. Not dating is a good idea for a few people—people who are vulnerable to destructive romantic fusion, who are being used by others, or who are avoiding maturity. Not dating is a good idea to give these people an opportunity to grow.

But, for others, we think dating can be a very good experience. And so does Harris. He just doesn't call it "dating." He says that a couple should spend time with each other to see if they are right for one another before they go forward into marriage. But, he distinguishes that from dating because from the first "date," the couple is investigating marriage. Up until this point, there was friendship. Not a bad plan, we believe. Get to know someone well before you commit to marriage. We also believe that dating offers this opportunity—and more.

Here are a few of the benefits we see in dating:

1. *Dating gives people the opportunity to learn about themselves, others, and relationships in a safe context.*

When done properly, dating is an incubator time of discovering the opposite sex, one's own sexual feelings, moral limits, one's need for relationship skills, and one's tastes in people. But dating must be done in the proper context. A single person must date within a community of people who care about him or her. For teens, this context is their parents, friends, youth group, youth pastor, coaches, and the like.

Dating gives people a place to grow and learn in the safety of people who can help them develop. I told one youth worker who believed in the no-dating movement that I thought he was robbing teens of needed input and coaching if he encouraged them to not date. I would rather see teens learn in a situation where they have guidance and have an opportunity to mature before making a marriage commitment than see them make a commitment and then have to figure all of that out later.

The same is true for older singles. Their friends, pastors, and community should provide support for their dating lives. This gives them a place to grow until they are ready for marriage.

2. *Dating provides a context to work through issues.*

Ask some happily married people how they would have fared if they had married their first boyfriend or girlfriend. We have all seen it a thousand times. People's first choices of who they are attracted to may not be so great. Dating offers people a place to find out that what they think they value in a person might not be what they value in the long term. They may find that what they are attracted to is fleeting and can even be destructive. Some of these attractions can even take on spiritual overtones. I have heard many times that someone was attracted to another person's spiritual "maturity" and character. They thought the person was great. But after they started to date, they got to know him or her a lot better, and closer. And they found out that what looked so good in a casual relationship did not hold water in a closer relationship over time.

I was talking to a woman who had grown up with an overpowering father and who had a strong dislike for this domination. She was attracted to men who were kind and soft, qualities her father did not possess. She ended up marrying her first boyfriend, after dating for only a short while. He was a very nice and kind man, but because she feared a man's power, a very passive one. She was sorry that she did not learn earlier about her tendency to idealize passivity. Had she dated her husband for a while, she would have known what she was getting into and what he was like in a real relationship. Lots of people look good until there is a real relationship day after day.

3. *Dating helps build relationship skills.*

Intimate relationships take a lot of work and a lot of skills. Many people do not come to the table of adulthood having learned these relationship skills in their families or other places. But, when they begin dating, they find out that they possess some serious insecurities, or they lack certain relationship skills, such as communication, vulnerability, trust, assertiveness, honesty, self-sacrifice, and listening. In their dating relationships they become aware of their immaturity and are able to find out what they need to work on before they are ready for a significant relationship. In addition, dating gives a person the opportunity to learn about relationship itself and how they function in a relationship. It can be an enormous time of growth and discovery.

4. *Dating can heal and repair.*

I ran into a man I hadn't seen in some time and was surprised to find that he was happily married to someone other than the woman he had been with when I had last seen him. When I asked him about his former girlfriend, he replied, "Oh, we are great friends, and I am so grateful to God for the role she played in my life."

"What do you mean?" I asked.

"For a while I thought she was the 'one.' But God had other plans long term for both of us. I do believe, however, that he brought us together for a season to teach us both a lot about ourselves and to bring about some healing. I had had so much hurt in the past, and she was so accepting and nurturing. Her love was very important to my becoming someone who could love again. Although I now know she was not the right one for me to marry, our relationship was really good for both of us and prepared us for future relationships."

God uses relationships to heal us and to change us. Although we are not suggesting that dating be the primary place that someone seeks healing (this is a horrible idea), it is a place where good things happen in people's souls. People benefit from good relationships. People can have good dating relationships where they learn, are healed, grow, and are stretched, even when the relationship does not lead to marriage. It has value in a person's life.

5. *Dating is relational and has value in and of itself.*

Joshua Harris says that people seek their own gratification in dating. While some people certainly use others selfishly in the dating realm, others enjoy getting to know another person, and they give and receive in a godly way, just not in a way that leads to marriage.

Getting to know someone, spending time with him, and sharing things with him is "intimacy." This knowing another person deeply is love. It is relationship, and it is holy and good. But in dating it is not *complete*. People who are not married do not give parts of themselves; they restrain from sexual union, for example. But, their other sharing has real value and is a wonderful thing, for no other reason than the love and relationship itself. It is its own end. God has said that love—and not just married love—is the fulfillment of the entire law. When two singles love each other, give to each other, and share something in life, although the relationship has limits of both body and heart, it has value as well.

6. *Dating lets someone learn what he or she likes in the opposite sex.*

We mentioned a woman above who would have done well to find out in dating that "nice" was not all it was cracked up to be. But there are other things people need to learn that are not based in this kind of pain. In her case, she was making up for her father's problems. Other people just do not know what kind of person they might really like and be good with. Everyone has some ideals and some natural attractions. Some of those may be good, and some may be rooted in sickness.

Not everyone knows what people he likes and what people are good for him. What is it like to spend a lot of time with a driver personality? For some it is heaven, for others, hell. What is it like to be around an intellectual person day after day? For some, it may be very stimulating. For others, very dry and boring. And we could go on and on. What we sometimes think we like is not what would really be good for us long term, but we have to find this out. Dating gives people a context to meet and spend time with a wide variety of people. They can find out what they like, what they need, and what is good for them.

7. Dating gives a context to learn sexual self-control and other delay of gratification.

Good dating allows people the opportunity to have a relationship and forgo sex. This delaying of gratification teaches something very valuable for marriage: the relationship and doing the best for the other person is more important than self-gratification and sexual expression. Some married couples do not know how to relate, and one or both use sex to substitute for relationship. Dating within God's limits makes people learn how to relate to one another while denying sexual expression. Dating done correctly teaches self-control and delay of gratification. Both of those are prerequisites for any marriage to work.

Dating can be done poorly and can lead to hurt and pain. Dating can be done well and can lead to wonderful fruits in the life of the teen and the adult single. *Boundaries in Dating* is designed to help you find the secrets of dating successfully and avoid the pitfalls of dating poorly.

If you will take this book seriously, seek God as deeply as you know how, establish a healthy community of friends to support you in the process, then dating can be something wonderful indeed. It can be fun, spiritually fulfilling, and growth producing. Keep your boundaries, and enjoy the process. Get involved in life, but remember God's boundaries and the way that he wants you to live a fulfilled, but holy life. It was expressed well in Solomon's advice to the young man (which also applies to young women): "Rejoice, young man, during your childhood, and let your heart be pleasant during the days of young manhood. And follow the impulses of your heart and the desires of your eyes. Yet know that God will bring you to judgment for all these things" (Ecclesiastes 11:9).

Dating can be a great time of life, but it must be balanced with God's boundaries of what is good. We hope that this book helps you find that safety, fulfillment, growth, and freedom.

Part One

You and
Your Boundaries

Chapter 1

Why Boundaries in Dating?

So what do I do, set a bomb underneath his chair?" Heather exploded, only partly in jest. She was having lunch with her best friend, Julie. The conversation focused on her ongoing frustration with Todd, Heather's boyfriend for the past year. Heather cared deeply for him and was ready to pursue marriage. Though he was loving, responsible, and fun, Todd had shown no sign of making any real commitment to the relationship. The couple enjoyed being together, yet anytime Heather tried to talk about getting serious, Todd would make a joke or skate around the issue. At thirty-three, Todd valued his freedom and saw no reason for anything in his life to change.

Heather's outburst was a response to something Julie had said: "You really need to help Todd get moving forward." Heather's words were tinted with frustration, hurt, and a good deal of discouragement. Frustration because she and Todd seemed to be on different tracks. Hurt because her love felt unrequited. And discouraged because she had invested so much of her heart, time, and energy into the relationship. For the past year, Heather had made Todd a high emotional priority in her life. She had given up activities she enjoyed; she had given up relationships she valued. She had tried to become the kind of person she thought Todd would be attracted to. And now it looked like this investment was going nowhere.

No Kids Allowed

Welcome to dating. If you have been in this unique type of relationship, you are probably familiar with Heather and Todd's scenario. Two people are genuinely attracted to each other and start going out. They are hopeful that the relationship will become something special that will lead to marriage and a life-long soul mate. Things look good for a while, but somehow something breaks down between them, causing heartache, frustration, and loneliness. And, more often than not, the scenario repeats itself in other relationships down the line.

Some people blame dating itself for all of this, thinking that it's not a healthy activity. They would rather find an alternative, such as group friendships until two people have selected each other to court exclusively. Though dating has its difficulties, we would not take this view. We believe in dating. We did it a lot personally, having been single a combined total of seventy-five years. And we think it offers lots of good things, such as opportunities to grow personally and learn how to relate to people, for starters.

However, dating does have its risks. That is why we say, *no kids allowed.* That doesn't mean teens shouldn't date, but it does mean one's maturity is very important here. By its very nature, dating is experimental, with little commitment initially, so someone can get out of a relationship without having to justify himself much. Putting lots of emotional investment into a relationship can be dangerous. Thus, dating works best between two responsible people.

Problems in Freedom and Responsibility

This book is not about the nature of dating, however. You cannot do a lot about that. Rather, we are writing about the problems people have in how they conduct their dating lives. There is a great deal you can do about that.

Simply put, many of the struggles people experience in dating relationships are, at heart, *caused by some problem in the areas of freedom and responsibility.* By freedom, we mean your ability to make choices based on your values, rather than choosing out of fear or guilt. Free people make commitments because they feel it's the right thing to do, and they are wholehearted about it. By responsibility, we mean your ability to execute your tasks in keeping the relationship healthy and loving, as well as being able to say no to things you shouldn't be responsible for. Responsible people shoulder their part of the dating relationship, but they don't tolerate harmful or inappropriate behavior.

Dating is ultimately about love. People seek it through dating. When they find it, and it matures, they often make deep commitments to each other. Freedom and responsibility are necessary for love to develop in dating. When two individuals allow each other freedom and take ownership of the relationship, they are creating an environment for love to grow and mature. Freedom and responsibility create a safe and secure environment for a couple to love, trust, explore, and deepen their experience of each other.

Actually, these two elements are necessary for any successful relationship, not just dating. Marriage, friendship, parenting, and business connections depend on freedom and responsibility in order for the attachment to flourish. God designed love so that there can be no fear (loss of freedom) in love, for perfect love casts out fear (1 John 4:18). We are to speak the truth in love to each other (Ephesians 4:15), taking responsibility to protect love by confronting problems.

We believe that healthy boundaries are the key to preserving freedom, responsibility, and ultimately love, in your dating life. Establishing and keeping good limits can do a great deal to not only cure a bad relationship, but make a good one better. So, before we take a look at the ways that dating problems arise from freedom and responsibility conflicts, let's take a brief look at what boundaries are and how they function in your dating relationships.

What Are Boundaries?

You may not be familiar with the term *boundary*. For some people, *boundaries* may bring up images of walls, barriers to intimacy, or even selfishness. Yet that is not the case, especially in the dating arena. If you understand what boundaries are and do, they can be one of the most helpful tools in your life to develop love, responsibility, and freedom. Let's take a look at what a boundary is, its functions and purpose, and some examples.

A Property Line

Simply put, a boundary is a *property line.* Just as a physical fence marks out where your yard ends and your neighbor's begins, a personal boundary distinguishes what is your emotional or personal property, and what belongs to someone else. You can't see your own boundary. However, you can tell it is there when someone crosses it. When another person tries to control you, tries to get too close to you, or asks you to do something you don't think is right, you should feel some sense of protest. Your boundary has been crossed.

The Functions of Boundaries

Boundaries serve two important functions. First, they *define* us. Boundaries show what we are and are not; what we agree and disagree with; what we love and hate. God has many clear boundaries. He loves the world (John 3:16); he loves cheerful givers (2 Corinthians 9:7). He hates haughty eyes and a lying tongue (Proverbs 6:16–17). As people made in his image, we also are to be honest and truthful about what we are and are not.

Dating goes much better when you are defined. When you are clear about your values, preferences, and morals, you solve many problems before they start. For example, a woman may tell a guy she is going out with that she is serious about her spiritual life, and desires that in people she is close to. She is letting him know about something that defines her, and it is out front between them, so that he will know who she is.

The second function of boundaries is that they *protect us.* Boundaries keep good things in, and bad things out. When we don't have clear limits, we can expose ourselves to unhealthy and destructive influences and people. Prudent people see danger and hide from it (Proverbs 27:12). For example, a man and woman who are getting closer in their relationship may want to set some limits on dating other people, so as to protect each other's hearts from unnecessary harm. Boundaries protect by letting others know what you will and will not tolerate.

Examples of Boundaries

There are several kinds of limits we can set and use in dating, all depending on the circumstances. Here are a few:

- Words: telling someone no and being honest about your disagreement
- The truth: bringing reality to a problem
- Distance: allowing time or physical space between two people to protect or as a consequence for irresponsible behavior
- Other people: using supportive friends to help keep a limit

Sometimes you will use these boundaries to simply let your date know your heart: "I am sensitive and wanted you to know that, so that we can be aware that I might get hurt easily." At other times, you may need to use boundaries to confront a problem and protect yourself or the relationship: "I will not go as far as you want sexually, and if you continue pushing, I will not see you again." Either way, boundaries give you freedom and choices.

What's Inside Your Boundaries

Remember that boundaries are a fence protecting your property. In dating, your property is your own soul. Boundaries surround the life God has given you to maintain and mature, so that you can become the person he created you to be. Here are some of the contents of your self that boundaries define and protect.

- **Your love:** your deepest capacity to connect and trust
- **Your emotions:** your need to own your feelings and not be controlled by someone else's feelings
- **Your values:** your need to have your life reflect what you care about most deeply
- **Your behaviors:** your control over how you act in your dating relationship
- **Your attitudes:** your stances and opinions about yourself and your date

You and only you are responsible for what is inside your boundaries. If someone else is controlling your love, emotions, or values, they are not the problem. Your inability to set limits on their control is the problem. Boundaries are the key to keeping your very soul safe, protected, and growing.

You will find many, many examples and situations in this book about how to apply boundary principles in your dating life. Just remember that you are not being mean when you say no. Instead, you may be saving yourself or even the relationship from harm.

How Boundary Problems Show Themselves

There are lots of ways that dating suffers when freedom and responsibility are not appropriately present. Here are a few of them.

Loss of Freedom to Be Oneself

Sometimes, one person will give up her identity and lifestyle to keep a relationship together. Then, when her true feelings emerge, the other person doesn't like who she really is, having never been exposed to her real self. Heather, in the introductory illustration, had lost some of her freedom in this way.

Being with the Wrong Person

When we have well-developed boundaries, we are more drawn to healthy, growing people. We are clear about what we will tolerate and what we love. Good boundaries run off the wackos, and attract people who are into responsibility and relationship. But when our boundaries are unclear or undeveloped, we run the risk of allowing people inside who shouldn't be there.

Dating from Inner Hurt Rather Than Our Values

Boundaries have so much to do with our values, what we believe and live out in life. When our boundaries are clear, our values can dictate what kinds of people fit the best. But often, people with poor boundaries have some soul-work to do, and they unknowingly attempt to work it out in dating. Instead of picking people because of their values, they react to their inner struggles and choose in some devastating ways. For example, the woman with controlling parents may be drawn to controlling men. Conversely, another woman with the same sort of background may react the opposite way, picking passive and compliant men so as to never be controlled. Either way, the hurt part inside is picking, not the values.

Not Dating

Sadly, some people who really want to be dating are on the sidelines, wondering if they will ever find anyone, or if anyone will find them. This is often caused by boundary conflicts, when people withdraw to avoid hurt and risk, and end up empty-handed.

Doing Too Much in the Relationship

Many people with boundary problems overstep their bounds and don't know when to stop giving of themselves. They will put their lives and hearts on hold for someone, only to find out that the other person was willing to take all that, but never really wanted to deeply commit. Good boundaries help you know how much to give, and when to stop giving.

Freedom without Responsibility

Freedom must always be accompanied by responsibility. When one person enjoys the freedom of dating, and takes no responsibility for himself, problems occur. Someone who is "having his cake and eating it too" in his dating relationship is in this category. This is Todd's situation. He enjoyed Heather but didn't want to take any responsibility to develop the relationship, though a great deal of time had passed.

Control Issues

More often than not, one person wants to get serious sooner than another. Sometimes in this situation, the more serious person attempts to rein in the other person by manipulation, guilt, domination, and intimidation. Love has become secondary, and control has become primary.

Not Taking Responsibility to Say No

This describes the "nice guy" who allows disrespect and poor treatment by his date, and either minimizes the reality that he is being mistreated, or simply hopes that one day she will stop. He disowns his responsibility to set a limit on bad things happening to him.

Sexual Impropriety

Couples often have difficulty keeping appropriate physical limits. They either avoid taking responsibility for the issue, or one person is the only one with the "brakes," or they ignore the deeper issues that are driving the activity.

There are many more ways that dating can become misery because of freedom and responsibility problems. We will go over many of them in the book. And, as you will see, understanding and applying boundaries in the right ways can make a world of difference in how you approach the dating arena.

In the next chapter, we will look at the first and foremost boundary line of any relationship: truth.

Take-Away Tips

- Dating involves risks, and boundaries help you navigate those risks.
- Boundaries are your "property lines" which define and protect you.
- Learn to value what your boundaries protect, such as your emotions, values, behaviors, and attitudes.
- Boundaries help you be yourself, instead of losing yourself in someone else.
- You want the person you date to take responsibility for his life, as you do.
- Good boundaries will help you choose better quality people because they help you become a better person.

——— *Chapter 2* ———

Require and Embody Truth

---

*J*went to a conference a few years back on working with character disorders, and the instructor was giving a list of priorities to psychologists who treat them. Character disorder is a catch-all term, but one way of defining it is people who do not take ownership and responsibility for their lives. I will never forget what the instructor said about the number-one priority—other than protecting your personal safety—in treating character disorders.

As soon as there is any kind of deception, stop everything. If you are trying to help someone and he is lying to you in some way, there is no relationship. The whole thing is a farce, and you should not go any further in trying to help the person until you settle the issue of deception. There are no other issues at that point except that one. Trust is everything in a helping relationship, and when it is broken, it becomes the only issue to work on. Either fix that or end the relationship. *Where there is deception there is no relationship.*

It was wise training and good counsel from a very experienced leader in the field. Thirty-five years of practice had taught him through experience that "where there is deception, there is no relationship." Truthfulness is everything. While essential in the therapeutic relationship, honesty is the bedrock of dating and marriage as well.

Standing on Quicksand

I was listening to a client tell her story the other day. Her marriage was torn asunder by an affair. The interesting thing, though, was that the marriage was not ripped by the affair, but by the lying. The husband had confessed some things to his wife and she was devastated. They separated for several months while she went through all of the pain associated with that kind of betrayal. Then, after all of that, she decided that she wanted to reconcile and get back together. She was softening and opening up, and he was repentant. Then she found out that he had not told her the whole story the first time and that things were worse than she had been led to believe.

The second deception was worse than the first. It was like the affair had happened all over again, except this time there was lying on top of the first lying and deception of it all. It was more than she could take. Feeling like she was standing on quicksand, she started the separation all over again. Her situation reminded me again of the wise psychiatrist's words, "*Where there is deception, there is no relationship.*"

I have seen deception undermine relationships in the areas of finances, work performance, substance use, and many other topics. The context changes from relationship to relationship, but the lying and deception are just as destructive no matter what topic someone is lying about. The real problem is that when you are with someone who is deceptive, you never know what reality is. You are not standing on firm ground, and the ground can shift at any moment. As one woman said, "It makes you question everything."

Deception in Dating

There are many different ways to deceive someone in the world of dating. Let's look at some of the more common ones.

Deception About Your Relationship

Karen liked Matt a lot, but after a few months of dating, she realized that the relationship was not going anywhere long-term. She liked "having him around," but Matt was getting more serious than she was in his feelings for her. He had stopped going out with other people and was beginning to treat her like a real girlfriend.

At first she was uncomfortable with his seriousness, but she tried to ignore the feeling. After all, she was having fun and did not see any harm in continuing to go out. But he was getting more and more affectionate, and there were other signs that he was "getting hooked." The more he did, the more she denied her awareness that she was not being straightforward. "What's the harm?" she convinced herself.

Then one night they were watching late-night TV when he leaned over and kissed her. He said softly, "I love you."

Karen felt her whole body go stiff. But she kissed him back and acted as if nothing was wrong. A little while later, she said she was tired and wanted to go to bed. She bid him good night, and he left.

Matt left on a high. He felt as if they had entered a new level of relationship. He had plans for their future and was a changed man. That night, he fell asleep dreaming of being together.

Where do you think the relationship went from there? There were two options. One was that Karen could call Matt the next day and say, "We need to talk. Last night when you said you loved me, it made me uncomfortable. I don't think that we are having the same sort of feelings for each other. I don't think that we are headed in the same direction, and I think we should just be friends."

Unfortunately, that is not what happened. She ignored her discomfort and continued to go out as if nothing was different. He continued to fall for her and she continued to allow him to do so. He took her to wonderful places and events, gave her lots of time and attention, and pursued her, all along the way thinking that they were boyfriend and girlfriend. And she allowed it. She enjoyed being with him, but had to ignore the slow split that was developing inside of her between the way that she was acting and the way that she knew she was feeling. But, she told herself, "He really is fun to be around. What's the harm in continuing to date?" And she did for a while, until she wanted to move on, and she felt that Matt was somewhat in the way. So, she finally had to tell him that she wanted to stop dating. She was not feeling "like the relationship was going anywhere," she told him.

Matt was devastated. He could not believe it. One day they were an item, and the next they were finished. How could this have happened? Disillusioned, he did not date again for a long time.

Many singles have found themselves on one side or the other of Matt and Karen's situation. Either side is painful, but certainly Matt had the worse end of things. He was being deceived into thinking that things were a certain way when they were not. And his heart was responding to what he perceived reality to be. In the end, he was really hurt. — lied to him

Hurt, and often loss, comes with dating. Losing a love or the hope of love is part of the dating situation. But, while losing a love that one desires is almost inevitable in the dating life at some time or another, *losing one's trust in the opposite sex does not have to happen if people are honest with one another*. As Paul says, "Therefore each of you must put off falsehood and speak truthfully to his neighbor, for we are all members of one body"

(Ephesians 4:25). It is one thing to have loved and lost. It is another thing to have loved and been lied to.

There is nothing wrong with dating someone, enjoying their company, and finding out where a relationship is going to go. That is almost a definition of the dating circumstance. But as soon as someone is sure that dating is not going where another person thinks or hopes that it is, that person has a responsibility to tell the other one clearly and honestly. Anything less is deceitful and harmful. *Do not lead someone on, or allow them to deceive themselves by anything that you are doing.* Matt would have been a lot better off if he had been hurt earlier, as soon as Karen knew what was happening. That might have increased his trust of women. But the opposite happened.

Deception About Being Friends

The same thing can happen in the opposite direction. While Karen was acting like a girlfriend when in reality she was just a friend, there are those who are deceptive about their true intentions while they are acting like a friend. These are people who have a secret crush and do all sorts of things for someone. Oftentimes they go way out of their way to help or minister to someone, but all along the way, they have ulterior motives. Then, when the "target" does not return the affection, they feel hurt and act like a victim, as if the target had done something horrible. All along the way, the target thought that they were "just friends."

There is nothing wrong with being friends and getting to know another person to see what kind of relationship you are going to have. Sometimes relationships that begin as friendships turn into more and are some of the best long-term relationships. But that is different than having clear designs on someone and deceiving them long-term while you have another agenda.

Certainly you don't have to put all of your cards on the table very early when you have a crush on a person. But devious designs and appropriate shrewdness are two very different things. Don't act like a friend that you are not. The best way to tell is to ask yourself, "What will happen if this does not end like I desire?" If you can honestly say that you will be very happy continuing to be friends and will love the person as a friend, then you are being honest. If you say, "If they do not want me back like I want them, I do not care about being 'friends' at all," then your friendship is a scam. Only you know for sure.

Deception About Other People

Sometimes people deceive each other about the nature of other people in their lives. They may act like someone is "just a friend," when there is more of a history, or more in the present than is being said.

I was working with a man who was trying to figure out his relationship with the woman he was dating, and he continued to have a funny feeling that something was wrong. It seemed that she was just a little too connected to her work. He had no problem with her loving her job, but there was something strange about her relationship with her boss. He did not think that she was dating him, or having any kind of illicit thing going on with him, but he still got a funny feeling about her work and her connection with her boss.

Finally he found out that his girlfriend had once been engaged to her boss. And there was still some sort of continuing tie between them. But, as far as he had known, it was strictly a work relationship. She had misled him.

He felt horribly deceived, and from there the relationship went downhill. It did not falter because she worked with a former boyfriend, but because she had not been clear about the nature of her former relationship with her boss. He could sense some sort of tie that she was not owning up to. Later, when some other issues came up where she had not been clear with him, the relationship died. If she had not been deceptive about the former boyfriend, the later issues would not have been a big deal. But once a pattern of deception is begun, trust is difficult to reestablish. (A footnote: she soon was back with the former boyfriend. I told my client I thought he was lucky to have escaped her.)

Deception About Who You Are

In a chapter about honesty, it is really important to remember that *you will have a good relationship to the degree that you are able to be clear and honest about everything*.

If you like a certain kind of music, church, movie, or activity, say so. If you don't want to go to a certain kind of event or outing, be honest. That does not mean that you cannot die to your own wishes to please someone else. But it does mean that you are not afraid to be yourself. Otherwise, the person will think you are different than you are, and there will be trouble later. In addition, compliant people have a habit of attracting controlling, self-centered people anyway, and you do not want to do that. Be honest, have some differences, and enjoy the trip.

Deception About Facts

There are people who tell lies not about feelings, relationships, or personal preferences, but about reality itself. Be careful of the following factual lies:

- Lying about whereabouts
- Lying about finances
- Lying about substance abuse
- Lying about seeing or being with someone else
- Lying about their past
- Lying about their achievements
- Other facts

When you catch the person you are dating in any kind of lie, see that as a character issue that you should take as a very solemn warning. Lying about reality places your relationship on a very shaky foundation.

Deception About Hurt and Conflict

We are assuming that you are going to tell the truth about the above areas, right? It is the other person you have to watch out for! But this section is especially for you, because if you lie in this area, you have no hope of finding out what kind of person you are really dating.

One of the most important things that you can do in a dating relationship that is getting anywhere near serious is to be honest about hurt and conflict. If you are dating someone, and there is a problem in some way that he or she has treated you, or some hurt that you have suffered, *you must be honest.* There are two important reasons you need to be honest about conflict:

1. Being honest resolves the hurt or the conflict.
2. When you are honest, how the other person responds tells you whether a real, long-term, satisfactory relationship is possible.

If you are hurt in some way, bring it up. Don't harbor bitter feelings. Or, if there is something that the other person has done that you do not like, or goes against your values, or is wrong, it must be discussed. If you don't you are building a relationship on a false sense of security and closeness, and it is possible that your feelings will be confused by hurt and fear. A lot is lost in not finding out who the other person is and where the relationship could really go, if one or both people are not facing hurt and conflict directly. In reality, a conflict-free relationship is probably a shallow relationship.

Second, you need to find out if the person you are with is capable of dealing with conflict and hurt directly. The Bible and all relationship research is very clear on this issue: *people who can handle confrontation and feedback are the ones who can make relationships work*. You must find out now, before it is too late, if the person you are with is someone you can talk to. If you get serious with someone who cannot take feedback about hurt or conflict, then you are headed for a lifetime of aloneness, resentment, and perhaps even abuse.

Proverbs puts it well about a person who cannot take confrontation: "Do not rebuke a mocker or he will hate you; rebuke a wise man and he will love you" (Proverbs 9:8). "A mocker resents correction; he will not consult the wise" (Proverbs 15:12).

You need to know if you are in a relationship with someone who is going to be defensive when you bring up hurt or conflict, or if you are with someone who is going to be able to listen, learn, and respond. If you do not deal with conflict now, and the relationship gets serious, then you have bought yourself a world of trouble.

Honesty over hurt and conflict creates intimacy, and it also divides people into the wise and the foolish. But being honest is totally up to you. What the person you are dating does you cannot control. But you can decide what kind of person you are going to be, and as a result, you will also be deciding what kind of person you are going to be with.

Two Types of Liars

Why do people lie, and what can you do about it? In our opinion, there are really two categories of liars. First, there are liars who lie out of shame, guilt, fear of conflict or loss of love, and other fears. They are the ones who lie when it would be a lot easier to tell the truth. They want to be honest, but for one reason

or another, cannot quite pull it off. They fear the other person's anger or loss of love.

The second category are liars who lie *as a way of operating*
and deceive others for their own selfish ends. There is no fear
or defensiveness involved, just plain old lying for love of self.

You will have to ask yourself if you want to take the risk and
do the work if you are with the first type. There are people in the
first category who have never had a relationship where they felt
safe enough to be honest, and they tend to still be hiding. So they
lie to preserve love, or preserve the relationship, or avoid being
caught in something because of guilt or shame. They are not really
dangerous, evil characters, and sometimes when they find someone safe, they learn to tell the truth. This is a risk that some people want to take after finding out that deception has occurred. They
hope that the person will be redeemed by the grace and love that
they offer and will shoot straight with them from then on.

While we would not automatically recommend continuing a
dating relationship with this kind of person, sometimes there
is a good outcome. So we do not want to make a rigid rule. But
our feeling is that dating is not a place for you to rehabilitate
people. Rehabilitation should occur in that person's counseling,
recovery, discipleship, or some other context. For one thing, dating can become serious when your heart gets involved, and it
may even lead to marriage. Just because the person is lying out
of fear does not make it acceptable, and serious devastation
can occur even with fearful liars. No matter what the reason,
lying destroys. By and large, the best policy is to stay away from
those who lie for any reason.

We think you should spend your time and heart on honest
people. It is often too risky, from our perspective, to get involved
with the fearful liar. If the person gets better and comes back
repentant, that is one thing. But you should not think that you

are going to be the one who changes him or her if defensive lying is an ongoing pattern. There are some people who do this on occasion and confess it, and probably can be trusted over the long haul. But patterns of this type are problematic. Whatever you decide to do, whether you stick in there or not, make sure that you do not go further until the lying issue is forever and certainly in the past. Remember the words of the wise instructor: Do not go on to other issues until the lying is solved.

The second kind of liar is a definite no-go. Tell him or her good-bye and save yourself a lot of heartache. Perpetual liars are not ready for a relationship, no matter how much you are attracted to him or her. Run, run, run.

Truth: The Essential Boundary

We believe that truthfulness is the basis for almost everything. You should have an absolute zero-tolerance policy when it comes to deception. Lying should have no place in your life. Listen to King David's tough stance on lying: "No one who practices deceit will dwell in my house; no one who speaks falsely will stand in my presence" (Psalm 101:7).

Clear, straightforward, and rigid. *Do not tolerate lying*, period. That does not mean that if you are lied to once or deceived once that the relationship has to be over. Especially in the area of the person not being totally clear and direct about how he or she feels about certain preferences, or what his or her desires are. Probably every human being is growing in his or her ability to be direct and completely vulnerable with feelings and deeper things of the heart. People grow in that ability, and sometimes a dating relationship is one of the places where that happens. None of us is perfect and secure enough to never use the fig leaf.

But don't tolerate deception or lying when it happens. If your dating partner is not clear about feelings, thoughts, or some other indirect communication, demand it. Don't let it go. Make a rule. "I have to be with someone who is honest with me about what they are thinking or feeling." Although lying about thoughts or feelings is not an instant relationship breaker, it is a significant area to be dealt with. If it remains a pattern, it may indeed need to be a "deal-breaker."

The other areas we mentioned are more dangerous, however. If you are two-timed, lied to about facts, with a substance abuser in denial, or otherwise deceived, we caution you about going forward. You need to be very careful and have a very good reason for continuing on. Many times lying like this is indicative of a serious character problem that does not change without major hurt for many people along the way. You do not want to be one of those.

If someone goes through a deep spiritual conversion, repentance, or turnaround, and sustains it for a significant amount of time, then you might consider trusting again. But remember, lying is one of the most dangerous of all character problems, and without a significant reason for you to believe that change has happened, you are asking for trouble. Do not tolerate it. Remember, to the extent that you are being deceived, there is no relationship.

If you are lied to:

1. Confront it.
2. Hear the response and see how much ownership and sorrow there is for the lying.
3. Try to figure out what the lying means in the relationship. If the person is afraid, guilty, or fears loss of love by you, then work on that dynamic and try to determine if the character issue is changing with more safety. But be careful.
4. Look at the level of repentance and change. How significantly is the person pursuing holiness and purity? How internally motivated is he or she to get better?

5. Is the change being sustained? Make sure you give it enough time. Just hearing "I'm sorry" is not good enough.
6. Look at the kind of lying it was. Was it to protect him or herself or just to serve selfish ends? If it is the latter, face reality squarely that you are with a person who loves himself more than the truth and face what that means. If the former, think long and hard and have a good reason to continue.

You Get What You Deserve

Finally, if you don't want to be in a relationship with a liar, be an honest person yourself. First, be honest with yourself. It takes some self-deception to be with a liar long-term, and if you are with one, you might already be less than honest with yourself. You probably know some things about that person's character that you are not facing squarely. Don't lie to yourself.

But, as Jesus said, to see others clearly, you have to get the log out of your own eye first (Matthew 7:3–5). Stop lying. Be clear and honest about everything. That does not mean that you have to reveal all that you are thinking immediately. You do not have to talk about all of your feelings or intentions on the first date. You do not have to bring up every little offense. People who do those things are not very attractive.

But it does mean that in significant areas, and especially if a relationship is becoming one in which your heart is getting involved, you must not lie. You must not deceive. You must be direct and clear. If you don't, you will end up with someone who for some reason needed to be with a less-than-honest person. That means that by your lying you have attracted a person who desires to stay away from truth, and that is a scary thought indeed.

Be a person of the light, and people of the light will be drawn to you, and people of the darkness will not be able to tolerate the truth you embody. That is the best protection of all. As Jesus said, "This is the verdict: light has come into the world, but men loved darkness instead of light because their deeds were evil. Every-one who does evil hates the light, and will not come into the light, for fear that his deeds will be exposed. But whoever lives by the truth comes into the light, so that it may be seen plainly that what he has done has been done through God" (John 3:19–21).

If you are an honest person, you will more likely end up with an honest person. If you deceive yourself or others, deceivers will be drawn to you. Be light and attract light. That is the best boundary of all.

Take-Away Tips

- Honesty is the bedrock of any relationship, and dating is no exception. When deception appears, let that be a big warning sign. Put on the brakes.
- Do not lead someone on. That is deception.
- Be careful to be honest and pure about your intentions at the proper time. To act like a friend when you have other intentions could undermine the friendship.
- If an old relationship is in the picture, do not try to deceive. That will undermine trust.
- Being yourself is the most basic form of honesty. That includes revealing what you like and dislike as well as what hurts you or bothers you.
- If you do encounter deception, face it head-on. From that point on, make sure the person has come clean and that growth is happening, or you are setting yourself up for hurt.
- As a general principle, honesty finds honesty. The more honest you are, the greater the chance of finding truthfulness in others.

─── *Chapter 3* ───

Take God on
a Date

J (Dr. Townsend) was watching a Christian television show a few years ago. The host was interviewing a world-renowned musician whose career had not been identified with religion, only with his great talent. The host said how glad he was that the artist was a Christian, and asked him to tell the TV audience about how he came to faith. The musician said, "Well, I always knew there was somebody up there." "Fantastic!" applauded the host. "What a great testimony to the saving power of Jesus!"

I thought, *Could you be reading into those words what you want to hear?* I was not questioning the artist's faith—that's between God and him. I was questioning how the host interpreted his statement. It seemed that he so much wanted the musician to clearly be a Christian that whatever he said would have been fantastic.

This sort of thinking is also common in the dating arena. You get connected to someone you are really drawn to, and you hope against hope that God is a part of his life and of the life of the relationship. And sometimes your hope bends the realities of the situation.

Though that sort of attitude has its problems, there is also a lot of good in it. It is a very good thing to want the person you

49

are close to to also be close to God. It is good to want a spiritually based relationship. Your relationship with God is the deepest, most profound, and most important part of your soul. If relationship is about connecting all of ourselves to another, then the spiritual aspect is inconceivably significant. So we all yearn for a person that we can be one with, all the way down to the core self, where God resides also. In fact, God designed our need to connect. Jesus prayed that we would be one in the same way that he and the Father are one (John 17:11). Ultimately, that is the final purpose of the dating quest. Through many experiences, conversations, and questions, we settle in on a person who loves God as we do, one who can help us grow even closer to him. If we don't feel some sort of conflict or loss because our date isn't on the same spiritual wavelength, there is a problem in our own religious life. Something is broken.

At the same time, many of us have had the same problem as the host in the TV show. We desire God, and we desire a person. And we sometimes don't know if the desires are working together or not. It is difficult to know how to navigate through the spiritual dimension of dating. So many questions arise, such as:

- Is this the person God meant for me?
- Are we spiritually compatible?
- How do I bring God into the relationship the "right" way?
- How do we relate spiritually?
- What if we disagree spiritually?
- Am I in denial about the spiritual conflicts we might have?

Though this entire book is about a biblical view of boundaries in dating, this chapter deals in particular with these and other explicitly spiritual issues. As you address the issues here, you will be equipped to set boundaries which will deepen the spiritual part of your dating life.

Dating Right Side Up

The first thing to deal with is an appropriate stance on dating and your spiritual life. This stance can help solve many problems and answer many questions from the very beginning of your relationship. The stance has to do with how we view dating and the spiritual life. *The issue is not how to fit our spiritual life into our dating life; rather, it is how to fit our dating life into our spiritual life.* To try to interpret God in the context of dating is an upside-down way to look at the realities. Life and love are his gifts and under his domain. He is the author of all good things, including dating. The right-side-up approach is to bring dating before God and ask for his guidance. After all, the One who designed emotional connections knows best how they are best conducted, in a way that is satisfying for us and glorifying to him.

Some Christians who have taken this approach have concluded that dating is not a good Christian activity. While we would disagree with that conclusion, we would agree with one part of that thinking. It is good to offer our dating life as part of the living sacrifice that helps submit all aspects of our lives to God's order for our existence. The more our lives are surrendered to him, the more he is able to fashion our lives as we were meant to be: "For in him we live and move and have our being" (Acts 17:28).

Idolatry

The alternative to surrender in dating is idolatry. Though dating is a good thing, we can commit idolatry by demanding that dating bring us the love, fulfillment, or desire we want without allowing God to point the way. Dating brings up powerful emotions and needs, and so idolatry can become a reality. Many times a person will find her relationship with God taking some sort of a detour as her dating world becomes more involved. You may need to set boundaries on dating as an idol, to bring your life back around to God's way.

For example, sometimes a person will find his own relationship with God waxing or waning depending on his dating relationship. He will get excited about God because his date is, or he will have a peripheral connection with God, for the same reason. In this case, he is depending on his date to give him a relationship with God, rather than owning the relationship with God for himself.

The Bible teaches that marriage is a heavy life investment. Dating can be the same. That is why it is wise to ask God about the place of both for your life: "I would like you to be free from concern. An unmarried man is concerned about the Lord's affairs—how he can please the Lord. But a married man is concerned about the affairs of this world—how he can please his wife—and his interests are divided" (1 Corinthians 7:32–34).

Surrender is a first and necessary element of bringing dating in line with God. However, it is not the only one. Surrender brings us into proper alignment with God, so that many other things can happen that will grow us up.

The Fruit of Your Dating Relationship

Ask yourself how your dating relationship impacts your spiritual life. Does it bring you closer to God, or push you further away? Important relationships rarely keep us in neutral spiritually. They tend to do one or the other. Here are a few things to look for as a way to evaluate this question:

- Are you drawn to the transcendent God through that person?
- Do you have an alliance with the other person in your spiritual walks?

- Do you experience spiritual growth from interacting with that person?
- Does the other person challenge you spiritually, rather than you having to be the impetus?
- Is the spiritual connection based on reality? Is the person authentic as well as spiritual?
- Is the relationship a place of mutual vulnerability about weaknesses and sins?

Let's assume you've aligned yourself under the lordship of Christ. At this point, we want to look at several parts of dating and spirituality to help you define what your boundaries should be in this area.

What Needs to Grow?

It is a great experience to begin to unveil yourself to your date spiritually. As you become safer, you can share deeper parts of yourself, thereby growing closer to each other and to God. There are several aspects of your spiritual life that you will want to bring into the relationship: your faith story, values, struggles, spiritual autonomy, and friendships.

Let's look at each of these elements.

Faith Story

Every believer has a story of how their relationship with God began and developed. A person without a spiritual history probably doesn't have much of a spiritual present. On the other hand, a person who has charted her spiritual path is opening up to you a window into who she is as a person. Some people have had quite dramatic and miraculous experiences. Others have undergone painful losses and tragedies that God has sustained them through. Some have experienced much emotional and personal healing through God. Others have struggled through complex theological questions. Still others have found ways to minister and to serve those in need in Christ's name. Find out the twists and turns of each other's spiritual history.

Values

Your values are the architecture of who you are. They are comprised of what you believe is most important in life, and how you conduct your life in accordance with these beliefs. Values are sometimes worth living and dying for, and are certainly worth dating and breaking up over. That is why opening up about your values is so critical. Your values will cover many aspects of life, including:

- Theology
- Calling in life
- Relationships
- Job and career
- Finances
- Family
- Sex
- Social issues

Values are part of your life. Forge them out of what the Bible teaches. Make them part of your dating world. Ask questions and provide your stances. Figure out which values are deal breakers and which are not. Remember not to get committed to someone who is incompatible in major areas, trusting that they will see the light and change.

I know a man who felt called to full-time ministry. He fell in love with and married a woman who didn't feel called in that direction. They have not gone into professional ministry, though they are active in their local church. But they have had tremendous struggles. He resents the fact that she held him back from ministry. And she feels controlled by his insistence that they go into full-time ministry.

Remember: Values are a major part of dating.

Struggles

Failure, loss, and learning experiences are part of the life of faith. Anyone who has been a believer for any amount of time knows that the spiritual life involves a great deal of hurt, confusion, and mistakes. So, to know a person's spiritual walk is also to know the times they stumbled in the darkness.

A friend of mine had a history of attempting to portray the perfect Christian guy façade with his dates. His relationships never worked. Either the woman believed him, and he felt unknown, or she saw through him, and he felt condemned. He met a woman he really liked, and, after seeing her for some time, decided to take a risk.

He told her, "I want to let you know I can be sexually manipulative. In times past, I have pretended to be safe and caring so that a woman will feel more open to sexual intimacy. I have taken advantage of that. I know I have grown and changed in my relationship with God and dealt with my personal issues. But I know that that part of me still exists. I really care about you, and want to know you better. And I figured that you need to know about this, so that we can deal with the issue openly if it comes out."

He told me later that the woman was pretty blown away by his confession. But she respected his honesty about his struggle, and the evidence of his obvious care for her. That relationship did not make it to marriage, but it was for other reasons, not that struggle. My friend never regretted bringing her into his struggle. In fact, he told me his present dating relationships are much better because of his experience. He is more honest about where he is with God and his growth. He is picking better women to date, and the quality of his relationships has improved.

There is certainly nothing wrong with wanting to put your best foot forward in a relationship by bringing your better self

into the connection first. Knowing good things helps us tolerate knowing bad things later, as grace must precede truth. Also,
prematurely opening up about your struggle can be a problem,
if you don't know how safe the other person is. But ultimately,
*if you don't know your date's spiritual struggles, you can't hon-
estly say you know your date.*

Here are some of the struggles people who are dating can talk
about to each other:

- Periods of being unsure about God's care or existence
- Living life apart from God
- Spiritual adolescence, challenging everything you have
  been taught
- Times of self-absorption when you neglected your
  spiritual growth

If you are dating someone who says she has never faltered or
doubted, something is wrong. Either she is in serious denial, or
you need to wonder what she is doing with you! No one grows
without experiences of loss and failure. The Bible teaches that
mature people have lots of practice dealing with the good and
evil in life: "But solid food is for the mature, who by constant
use have trained themselves to distinguish good from evil"
(Hebrews 5:14).

Spiritual Autonomy

Now let's look at your present spiritual condition. How do you
and your date conduct your spiritual life? Is it alive and active,
or does it need resurrection? People who are trying to pull off
a successful dating relationship need to know that the other person is spiritually autonomous. That is, he has his own walk with
God that he pursues on a regular basis, regardless of his circumstances. Spiritual autonomy ensures that he does not look to you
to provide his religious direction or motivation. He had some-

thing serious going on with God before he met you, and if you don't marry, he will continue on with God.

Spiritual autonomy is a major issue in dating. Sadly, many people date and marry someone without this trait. At the time, things seem okay. He is excited about deepening his growth as long as she is. Or he will say that the relationship has helped him break out of a spiritual deadness or slump, and how glad he is to be back in his faith. Dating as a spiritual jump start is risky business, for it can mask apathy or disinterest, like the eager but shallow soil that Jesus spoke of (Matthew 13:20–21).

The nature of dating lends itself to this problem. When you begin dating, you are experiencing new things with someone, and there is excitement and hope in the air. Fresh starts in life are part of the experience. And some people who have no real spiritual root will confuse their attraction to their date with their attraction to God. But often, when the relationship is getting rocky, so does the other's connection with God. In a way, God is only a representative of the date; God does not exist as a strong presence in his own right. As a friend of mine expressed it, "Sometimes I wasn't sure who he thought the Messiah was, Jesus or me."

There are certainly exceptions to this. Sometimes people take root during dating and flourish spiritually. Or sometimes the "spiritual" person gradually loses interest in her own faith. We can't predict what God will do in someone's heart. But we can say that dating someone who has not owned her own spiritual walk is a big red flag.

The reality is, often the "spiritual" date is guilty of making up what she wants, and projecting an authentic desire for God into the other person that may not really exist, as in the example of the TV show host. It is difficult to be in a marriage in which you find out that the spiritual direction of things is entirely dependent on you, instead of having a soul mate to pull along with you.

Even more importantly, you need a date who is spiritually autonomous when you yourself fall. You will need someone who is depending on God and living his life in God's path for those times that you are weak, failing, and doubting. Nothing is worse than to be in dark spiritual waters with a person who is himself also drowning: "Pity the man who falls and has no one to help him up!" (Ecclesiastes 4:10).

Only time will tell whether your date is truly spiritually autonomous. If you are wondering about your date's spiritual autonomy, no amount of protestations of commitment and spiritual fervor will give you the assurance you need, without the ingredient of time. Don't rush if you are concerned about this issue.

Spiritual autonomy also has to do with what have traditionally been called the spiritual disciplines: regular reading of the Bible; a meaningful prayer life; church attendance; visible identification as a Christian; and a concern for the lost and suffering. Religious style and worship preferences vary, but these are the essential elements that identify someone who belongs to Christ.

Friendships

You can learn a lot about each other by the sort of friends you have. We tend to engage people based on our own needs and values. One's spiritual life becomes reflected in one's relationships as well. This does not mean that your date must have exclusively Christian friends. That might indicate some sort of a fear of dealing with the real world. In fact, if your date avoids certain types of legalistic or hypocritical Christians, that might be a sign of her spiritual health!

At the same time, having no lasting Christian friendships could mean problems. It might mean that she is just beginning her spiritual growth path. Or it could mean she has had a dry or stagnant season, and is now becoming reinvolved with the life of God. It could indicate that she has never had a deep spiritual life. Or it could mean that she is not a Christian, but rather a religious person who has never received Christ as her Savior.

These questions about friendships and one's spiritual condition are not meant to provide you with a judgmental scrutiny, but as ways for both of you to examine your hearts and your relationships with God and each other. The more you know about each other, the more you can see if you are good marriage material for each other.

Differences Can Promote Growth

Demanding that your date have exactly the same spiritual values as you could be a problem. Though the fundamentals of the Christian life, as we have outlined above, are basic requirements, it is best to be in relationship with someone who has thought through his own spiritual issues deeply and individually, and has reached his own conclusions. To require precisely the same theological or traditional values in all areas, large and small, could indicate control issues, perfectionism, or uncertainty in your own faith. Fall in love with someone who can take you on spiritually, and let the sparks fly! Some of the most meaningful times of growth for dates can be when they argue, read the Bible, and come to terms on spiritual matters.

Integration of Faith into Real Life

There are religious people, and there are spiritual people. Religious people know the Truth, but spiritual people do it. You want you and your date to have lives that reflect both knowing and doing spiritual reality in the real world. And that is what character is all about: integrating the realities of God's ordinances into everyday life.

God meant your spiritual life to drive and direct all other aspects of your life: relational, financial, sexual, job concerns, and everything else that comprises life. Too often, sincerely believing folks may read their Bibles and faithfully attend church, but at the same time, have great conflicts bringing their spiritual values into all of their existence. This problem occurs in two basic forms in the dating world: *difficulties in bringing up faith matters, and difficulties in living the life.*

Difficulties in Bringing Up Faith Matters

We don't believe you can only find people to date at church. There are plenty of deeply spiritual believers in all of the other arenas of life. They are the same arenas you live in: the business environment; hobby centers; sports; social work and care for the unfortunate; and others. If you want your date to be a person with a life, get out in life and look for him!

Unfortunately, this may mean you may not know much about a person's faith as you evaluate whether or not you want to pursue dating him. You can tell a lot about character by how a person operates in the world, but character maturity is not always derived from Christian belief. There are caring and responsible people who aren't believers. So it is important to address issues of faith pretty soon.

Some people have a lot of problems bringing up spiritual issues. They don't know where to start and feel a lot of conflict about it. Here are some of the problems:

- Feeling awkward and unnatural
- Not wanting to turn the date off to God
- Being anxious that you might lose the relationship
- Being concerned that since you aren't perfect, you'll be seen as hypocritical
- Not knowing how to discuss spiritual issues because they are so private

These are all important issues. However, it is helpful to remember the underlying reality of dating: you are ultimately trying to find and be a good marriage partner. You want that person to know about and share your relationship with God, because that is the most important part of who you are, and hopefully, of who he is.

Difficulties in Living the Life

So many folks in the dating world do talk about their faith with each other, and support each other spiritually. Yet they have another conflict: they have areas in their dating life where they don't "walk the talk." They exhibit a chronic pattern of weakness or struggle that doesn't seem to resolve itself over time. It may be sex, deception, immature ways of conflict resolution, or control issues. Whatever it is, their spiritual life has not transformed their character, as it should. There is a painful split, or contradiction, between what they believe and what they are practicing.

This split existence is often not the product of a lack of commitment to God. Indeed, they might be deeply spiritual. A split existence has more to do with their inability to integrate their needs and life into God's ways of meeting needs. Sexual acting out may be a shortcut to intimacy or other needs, as we will see in the chapter on physical relationships. Rescuing an immature date from the consequences of his bad temper may be due to a fear of being honest and righteous. Back-and-forth relationships that involve lots of breaking up and making up may be the symptom of an inability to emotionally leave home and be an independent adult.

I was having a business lunch with a man who did not know my faith. We were doing the usual kibitzing about our lives to get to know each other. This man spent a lot of time talking badly about his wife, as well as discussing lots of other women he was interested in in a sexual way. Somehow we got on religion, and I mentioned my faith. Immediately he also identified himself as a Christian, and began talking in glorious terms about the grace of God and his deep love for Christ. I wondered if I was with the same guy, so complete was his turnaround. But as I listened, the spiritual stuff sounded pretty canned, like a sermon that he had preached many times. I think he was probably a believer. But this man had the sort of split existence that makes life miserable. This is the sort of split that many people find in themselves or in their dates.

Whatever the cause, there are spiritual answers to these conflicts, and the couple needs to be dealing with these. That is why you want to be dating someone who is not only of the faith, but is aware of his or her weaknesses and issues, and is in the process of working things out, whether it be in accountability groups, support groups, or counseling. A lifetime of marriage to a person with a character issue that has never been addressed can be very painful.

This is why it is so important to speak up and address things that don't make sense to you with your date. If you notice inconsistency in him or in how the relationship is going, bring it up. If he is a goodhearted person, he will probably be grateful that you took a risk, and you both can work on resolving it. *Don't demand perfection in him or yourself. Instead, require righteousness.* A righteous person stays connected to God, his source. But when he slips and falls, he will take correction well and will reconnect himself back to God.

An Active Role in Each Other's Growth

Another aspect of the spiritual part of dating is that you need to matter to each other on a spiritual level. This tends to increase over time as the relationship deepens and is more committed, but the idea is that you need to be part of each other's growth and conduct. Even if you do not end up marrying, you need to take the stance that during your tenure as dates, you both will grow spiritually. Here are some of the ways you can help each other grow.

Input and Feedback

As your relationship grows, so should your awareness of each other's struggles and needs. Your date is in a unique position with you, and may know or see things in you that others do not see. In the more committed stages of the connection, you need to give each other permission to confront, give input, and encourage on spiritual levels. If your date is resistant to spiritual feedback, something is amiss, as the Bible has harsh words for those who can't handle input: "Whoever corrects a mocker invites insult; whoever rebukes a wicked man incurs abuse" (Proverbs 9:7).

Give It Time

Generally speaking, it is a good idea to let some time and experiences pass between you before confronting a great deal. Be "quick to listen, slow to speak" (James 1:19). You may have misunderstood something that you might see better over time. Or you might see an act that may never be repeated again, so that what you interpreted as a pattern was really an isolated event. Or you may need to let time pass for enough grace to build between you so that you won't be seen as a condemning judge. Remember that we all need grace before we hear truth.

Don't Be a Parent

Avoid the tendency to take the role of spiritual responsibility for your date. Don't set up the relationship so that she is performing and growing under your tutelage. Why? Because children have one main job, and that is to leave their parents. If you are the daddy, she must grow up and leave you in order to fulfill God's purpose of becoming an adult.

A friend of mine made this mistake. He fell in love with a woman whom he then began to disciple. He took her through various Bible studies, gave her assignments, and had her reading books. He was so excited about this until the day she left him for another guy, stating that she felt too controlled. It was a devastating experience for him. However, he learned from it. He told me, "Next time, I'll leave the discipling to someone else."

Comfort and Challenge

Good relationships involve not only feedback, but enough permission to comfort each other's hurts and challenge each other's failings. Make sure you are both doing both. Some relationships are strong on comfort, but there is no spurring each other on. And some are quite challenging, but can also be harsh and critical. Be both comforting *and* challenging.

Spiritual Compatibility

A major aspect of dating is spiritual compatibility, or the extent to which you are a good match in your faith lives. At one level, this should be an easy area to deal with. At another, it is a very difficult one.

The Design Issue

The easy part is that God has designed you for intimacy with himself and others. We can trust that this is part of our makeup. It also means that the deepest part of you is made to desire spiritual intimacy with another person. If that part of you is working properly, you will seek out healthy spirituality in others. Ultimately, you will be interested in and drawn to others who share your spiritual life. If something is broken inside, you will tend to find yourself drawn to unhealthy or absent spirituality. So at this level, spiritual compatibility is a diagnostic issue of our own spiritual health. However, there are other considerations.

Spiritual Development Path

Spiritual development means that you are not who you were, nor are you who you will be. With perseverance in the process,

we are ultimately to become mature and complete (James 1:4).
As you mature, your attitudes, values, and habits change. Sometimes people date and fall in love during a particular period of
spiritual growth for one or both. Things go well as long as both
are in the same period. However, if one of them goes through
major changes, there is a great deal of conflict and adjustment.

I knew a couple who were both going through a phase of spiritual adolescence and doubt. They were questioning God, the
church, the Bible, and dabbling in other faiths. Supporting each
other's quest and exploration, they married. However, the
woman subsequently returned to her Christianity, divested of
some of the traditions that had burdened her. But her husband
stayed on the fringes of faith and has never returned. Though
he is a good man in many other ways, she has had a very lonely
road in the spiritual part of her marriage.

Now, it is unrealistic to require that you and your dates all
be full-grown, as everyone will continue changing. But we would
be concerned if you or your date had never had a spiritually questioning period of some sort. Questioning is how people truly
"own" their faith, instead of piggybacking on the faith of their
parents. At the same time, it is important that both you and your
date have resolved the major tenets of your quest. Do not get
serious if your date is still up in the air about the content and
meaning of her Christianity. At a time of spiritual questioning
you can be supportive and helpful, giving room to grow, but
do not make major commitments.

Areas of Belief and Practice

As you get to know your date spiritually, you will need to
decide what areas of belief and practice are disagreements you
can live with, and those you can't. Some of this will be preference, and some will be pretty objective. The tenets of Christianity are well-articulated, and you need to know them for

yourself. Discuss and deal with these with your date, as you become closer.

Differences in Spiritual Level

Many people struggle with questions of dating others who are at a different level than they are spiritually. Here are some of the differences, and some suggestions on how to deal with them.

Christian and Non-Christian

Christians need to be very involved in the real world, as agents of God's love. This is what being salt and light are about (Matthew 5:13–16). At the same time, the deepest and most significant part of you needs to find a home in the heart of the most important human relationship in your life (2 Corinthians 6:14). Because of this, we believe that Christians should not be in serious dating relationships with non-Christians.

This is not to say that you should not have non-Christian friends of the opposite sex. Many enriching relationships can occur here, and non-Christians need to know that there are believing men and women who can treat them in respectful "brother-sister" ways. However, we believe that it is best to reserve your romantic interests for those of the same faith. Romantic desire is a wonderful gift. But it has been known to cloud the best judgment, and can unknowingly exploit our own character weaknesses. So connect your romantic parts to good-hearted believers in your faith, so that when you truly fall in love, that aspect won't be an issue.

Committed and Uncommitted

Many people who are serious about their faith wonder about dating Christians who are only peripherally involved in their spiritual life. This question is more complex than the above one. Here are some ways to think about it.

How do you know your date is uncommitted? First, make sure about what you are perceiving. Sometimes our own judgmentalism or perfectionism can make "different" seem "bad." The person may not seem to be on the same track, but she may have a much deeper track that you can't see because of your own issues. Do not assume, for example, that because she does not know the Bible as well as you that she does not love God as much as you.

Why does she seem less committed? Sometimes a person seems less committed because she has sustained loss, overwhelming stress, or failure in life. Though ideally we should become closer to God in these times, sometimes we withdraw. An otherwise deeply connected person may be going through a very bad time spiritually. In these cases, it is worth it to support her struggle and help her resolve it, while putting serious commitment on the back burner until things play themselves out.

What if she remains uncommitted? There certainly are believers who stay at lesser levels of commitment to God. If it becomes clear over time that this is the case, it is probably better to part ways. Again, this is one of those questions that is better solved by your own spiritual health. If things are working right inside of yourself, you will at some point sense a spiritual emptiness in the relationship that, when translated to marriage, can be a major problem.

Mature and New

This is a more complex issue. Suppose you are both pretty serious about your faith, but one has been in the growth process longer than another. Here are some ways to approach this scenario.

If you are a very new Christian (say, less than a year in the faith), congratulations and welcome to the family! We would suggest that you get involved in the spiritual growth process and become stable in your faith as you continue in your relationship. The object is to grow on your own spiritually, so that your faith is not dependent on your partner's.

If you are a more mature believer, it is again good to wait until the new Christian's faith has solidified before making deeper commitments. This keeps you out of the parent role and lets your date take more ownership over his growth process.

Don't go by time alone as you observe your spiritual issues. Though time is necessary, some people grow at faster rates than others. Don't assume that because someone has been around for a while, that they are mature. At the same time, the younger believer still needs time to develop and mature.

Ultimately, it is best to date those who are at about the same maturity level as you are. This can solve many dependency, control, and growth conflicts. But make sure that you are scrutinizing yourself harder than you are your date (James 4:6). And make sure that both of you are more interested in pursuing God and growth than you are in being at the same level! It is truly more important to be engaged in the process than it is to be constantly jockeying for position.

In addition, make sure what you see as a maturity difference is not simply a stylistic difference. This is like what we said about the commitment issue. A person who hasn't had formal theological training, for example, may be much more mature in her walk and character than someone who has. Remember that God cares more about our hearts than our religious traditions: "I desire mercy, not sacrifice" (Matthew 9:13). Always include character in how you approach each other. Look at whether the person loves, is truthful, lives in reality, and functions as an adult. Often, a person who functions well in the real world has a better adjusted spiritual life than someone who has a lot of head knowledge, but can't function as well.

Conclusion

Ultimately, the spiritual part of dating means we are to set limits on all sorts of desires and impulses:

- Wanting the person to be compatible spiritually, if he is not
- Trying to change the other person spiritually
- Denying spiritual conflicts in the relationship
- Missing our own spiritual weaknesses and focusing on our partner's
- Being afraid to address spiritual issues

However, as we continue to grow in Christ and his paths, it becomes easier to love and invest our hearts wisely and well in our dating lives.

Take-Away Tips

- Don't wait until later to make your faith part of your relationship. It is just as real to your life as your career and taste in movies.
- Don't interpret religious agreement or passivity on your date's part as spiritual compatibility. He or she should have an active faith that has involved thought and struggle. If you find yourself always taking the initiative, see that as a problem.
- Enjoy spiritual differences within our faith and learn from them. Don't beat up your date trying to convince her of a certain position.
- Develop a relationship in which you are both challenging each other to "walk your talk."

Chapter 4

Dating Won't Cure a Lonely Heart

*J*ust call him and tell him that it is over," I (Dr. Cloud) said to Marsha. I had listened to her for months now about her relationship with Scott and how she could not stand some of his hurtful patterns. And I was getting both concerned and tired of her denial of the kind of person that he really was. I began to push her.

So she decided to do it. She called him and broke it off. As expected, he went crazy and showed up at her door begging for her to not go through with it. There were all sorts of promises of change and the usual things that people in denial say when threatened with loss of love. But she held her ground. At least for a day.

Two days later, Marsha called and canceled her next appointment. I called her back and found out the truth. She had gone back to Scott and was ashamed to tell me. I told her to come in anyway so we could talk about it.

As Marsha talked, I felt for her. She described the depression and aloneness that she went into when she broke it off and held her ground. She felt as if she were in a black hole that she could not see out of, and she felt completely hopeless. It was really a dangerous state.

No one who knew Marsha would have suspected her inner agony. She was a strong person in the business world, a committed Christian, and a ministry leader in her church. Everyone loved her, and no one would have thought that she would put up with someone like Scott, or that she could be so devastated by breaking up with such a jerk. But the breakup had left her so sad that she could barely function.

As we worked on her feelings, we found that there was a very deep part of her that felt very much alone and unloved, and breaking up with Scott was bringing out a deep aloneness that normally she did not experience. And, as we began to look at her history, she avoided experiencing this internal aloneness by dating men. Each time she would end one relationship, there would be another one, even though they would not be men that she would want to be with long-term. She just could not stand to be alone. And so, her fear of being alone kept her from having boundaries with bad relationships. She would rather give in to a bad relationship than have no relationship at all.

This is a key point about boundaries in dating. If you do any of the following, then you might be giving up boundaries because of a fear of being alone:

- Putting up with behavior that is disrespectful
- Giving in to things that are not in accord with your values
- Settling for less than you know you really desire or need
- Staying in a relationship that you know has passed its deadline
- Going back into a relationship that you know should be over
- Getting into a relationship that you know is not going anywhere
- Smothering the person you are dating with excessive needs or control

And surely there are other signs as well. But the point is, your dating is ruled by your internal isolation, rather than by your God, goals, values, and spiritual commitments. Your aloneness makes you get involved in relationships that you know are not going to last. It also keeps you from being alone long enough to grow into a person who does not *have to be in a relationship* in order to be happy. There is a very important rule in dating and romance: To be happy in a relationship, and to pick the kind of relationship that is going to be the kind you desire, you must be able to be happy without one.

If you must be dating or married in order to be happy, you are dependent, and you will never be happy with whatever person you find. The dependency will keep you from being selective enough to find the kind of person who will be good for you, or will keep you from being able to fully realize a relationship with a healthy person. If you are afraid of aloneness and abandonment, you cannot use the love of people who are truly there until you deal with your own fears.

So, aloneness must be cured first, and this is a good boundary for dating. Here is the boundary: In order to cure your fear of being alone, you need to put a boundary around your wish for a relationship. *Cure that fear first*, and *then* find a relationship.

How do you cure your aloneness without a dating relationship?

First, strengthen your relationship with God. Make him your first priority so that you are not trying to get God needs met by a relationship with a person.

Second, strengthen your relationships with safe, healthy Christians. Make sure that you are not trying to get your people needs met by a dating relationship, or by God. Yes, you need God. But you also need people.

Dating is an adult relationship meant for mature, intact adults to engage in. And mature adults will always have a good support system that meets their needs for human contact. In addition,

mature adults are able to take their needs to others for healing. If you try to have a romantic relationship meet your needs
for healing, it is not going to work. You need a support system
to ground you so that you can make choices out of strength,
not weakness or dependency. Marsha was choosing men out
of her weakness, and thus could never find the kind of man she
wanted. If you have your needs met outside of dating, then you
can choose out of strength.

Be vulnerable in those support settings. Many people have
a lot of friends, but those friendships are not meeting their deepest needs. So they are still vulnerable to dependencies in dating.
Just because you have friends does not mean that you are being
healed. Make sure that in some of those relationships you are
allowing yourself to be dependent, have needs, express pain and
hurts, and the like. You may need to include counseling or a
counseling group as part of that support system. But a support
system is only going to do you as much good as you allow it to
by expressing your needs. This vulnerability will connect you
to where you can be strong enough and not lonely.

Have a full life of spiritual growth, personal growth, vocational
growth, altruistic service, hobbies, intellectual growth, and the
like. The active, growing life does not have time or inclination
to be dependent on a date. The more you have a full life of relationship with God, service to others, and interesting stimulating
activities, the less you will feel like you need a relationship in
order to be whole.

Pursue wholeness. In addition to an active life, work on the
issues that are in your soul. Whatever those issues are, as you are
resolving them (past childhood hurts, recurring themes and patterns in your relationships and work life, and other areas of brokenness, pain, and dysfunction), your aloneness will be cured
as well. It is a curious thing, but the process of spiritual growth
itself can help cure aloneness. As you grow spiritually, you are

going to naturally be closer to others and get a fuller life. The whole person is not a dating addict. He or she is happy and fulfilled. As Psalm 1:3 says of the person who is growing into all of God's ways and law: "He is like a tree planted by streams of water, which yields its fruit in season and whose leaf does not wither. Whatever he does prospers." The whole life is a full life. And the by-product of fullness is that the fulfilled person is also a very attractive one.

See if your fear of aloneness is pertaining to a specific issue. For example, Marsha, suffered abandonment as a child. Other people have to deal with unresolved losses of other kinds. There are many kinds of pain that drive fears of aloneness. See if your pain is specific to a particular thing that you have gone through in your life, and then work to resolve that issue.

The best boundary against giving in to bad relationships, less-than-satisfactory relationships, or bad dynamics in a good relationship is your not needing that relationship. And that is going to come from being grounded in God, grounded in a support system, working out your issues, having a full life, and pursuing wholeness. If you are doing those things, you will not be subject to saying yes when you should be saying no.

Take-Away Tips

- Dating was never meant to cure aloneness. It was meant to fulfill adult needs for male-female romantic relationship on the way toward marriage.
- Aloneness is to be cured by relationships with God and other people.
- These relationships will never help if you do not achieve vulnerability within them.
- A full life as a single will help you to not choose a relationship out of aloneness or lack of fulfillment.

- Choices made out of need are less than satisfactory or self-destruct.
- You must get to a place where you are happy with your life apart from a dating relationship in order to be happy with one.
- Symptoms of giving up your boundaries in many areas of dating may come from an underlying fear of being alone.

Chapter 5

Don't Repeat
the Past

In researching this book, I (Dr. Townsend) interviewed married as well as single friends to get their perspectives on the dating game. One question I asked married people was "Now that you're done with dating, what would you have done differently during those days?" The majority of responses were something like, "I would have learned more from my previous mistakes." That is an interesting answer. I think it means something like, "If I could do things differently, I would do things differently." People have many deep regrets, and wish they could have benefited more from their experiences.

It is important to set a boundary with your past, that is, to deal with your old dating patterns as something that you are not destined to continue. Your past can be your best friend or worst enemy in terms of helping you develop the right sort of dating relationships. No one enters the dating world competent and ready to go. You may come from a good family and relational background. You may be a well-rounded person. These are certainly advantages. But, even given these advantages, the specific arena of dating, like any other relational undertaking, must be experienced through hours and hours of trial and error.

The past is important because it is the repository of all those trial-and-error experiences. Your past can provide a great deal of necessary information on what to do and what to avoid in dating, either through the satisfaction of doing it right, or the pain of doing it wrong. To blithely skip over the past in an attitude of, *I don't need to think about it, it's all behind me, and tomorrow is a new day,* is to ignore important aspects of reality. On the other hand, to pay attention to what you have done before is to take ownership of your present and future, which you can do something about.

This chapter will deal with how your past affects your dating, and what you can do to make your past work for you, instead of against you. Do not let the past hinder and entangle you: "Let us throw off everything that hinders and the sin that so easily entangles, and let us run with perseverance the race marked out for us" (Hebrews 12:1).

Become a good historian of yourself.

Dating Patterns

You may wonder, *What specific past am I repeating in my dating relationships?* You will want to look for problematic patterns of dating that hinder progress toward depth, commitment, and marriage. In a way, this entire book is about the various dating problems people have encountered in the past, and how to deal with them. Some people have a tendency to go too quickly; some adapt to their date's desires; some allow the relationship to rule them; and so on. As you read through this book, you will want to take note of the patterns you identify with, then learn what you can to stop repeating the pattern.

What Can I Learn from the Past?

The first dating problem is denying that your past demonstrates a problem! You can't learn from the past if you believe the issue is solely the unsuitable people you have dated. If you are more concerned with them, it is their past you're dealing with, not yours. Instead of blaming your dating problems on the people you date, you need to become very curious and active in figuring out what your past dating approaches have been.

I have a friend who has been praying fervently for several years to find a husband. She is pretty frustrated with the failures of her relationships. But when I asked her recently what she thought the problem was, she said, "The guys aren't the right guys." I am not saying men are anything more than they are. But until my friend sees that *she* is the common denominator in all of these "wrong" guys, I don't see how things will change.

So if you tend to get with your buddies and have gripe sessions about the lack of quality dating material in the world, do something constructive for a change. Ask them, God, and yourself the same question: *What can I learn from my dating past that will help me avoid bad things or experience good things in the future?* This requires more work than griping, and is nowhere near as enjoyable, but it does tend to produce good results. An even more pointed question is, *What have I done to contribute to my dating problems today?* This is not about self-condemnation. Instead, it is about a quest for truth and reality, to free you up from repeating past mistakes.

Understanding the Past Helps Us to Grow

Jim had been a happy-go-lucky man in his twenties. He dated quite a bit, but nothing ever came of the relationships. However, Jim wrote it off to bad luck and comforted himself with the knowledge that he had lots of time to find someone. He never really sat down and wondered what was going on. Time, however, caught up with Jim. By his midthirties, he became concerned. He had always wanted to be married by then. Jim became anxious that he might never get married at all.

At this point, the older, wiser Jim slowed down a little and began seriously thinking about his dating pattern. He finally figured it out. Jim tended to go after women who wanted him more than he wanted them. The main thing he was attracted to was that a woman really liked him. It was less risky for him. However, once the relationship became more involved, he would quickly lose interest, as they were not what he desired in the first place. Almost every past relationship had this same clear progression. Jim was amazed when he put the pattern together. I was proud of Jim, because he worked very hard to diagnose the problem.

By this time, Jim had been dating two women, Robin and Jenny. He was honest about this with both women, and was not deceptive. Robin was very interested in him, which normally would initially render her more interesting to him. Jenny, on the other hand, liked Jim but wanted to keep dating other people. This was a struggle for him. The old Jim would have never pursued Jenny after a couple of dates, so great was his insecurity about taking risks with women.

Fortunately, Jim had been pondering his pattern of low-risk dating, and was willing to use his knowledge of the past. What Jim did was to bring his loneliness and insecurity out of his dating world and into his friendships. He opened up to his safe cluster of friends about his feelings, and took risks with them about how afraid he was of committing to them or anyone else. They stuck with him and supported him.

Eventually, Jim became more able to be honest and straightforward with people, secure in the knowledge that he had a solid foundation of relationship between God and a few good folks. In other words, Jim was growing. He got honest with Robin and told her he just didn't have enough interest to continue dating. And he pursued Jenny, though it almost gave him panic attacks to go after such an unsure deal.

As it happened over time, Jim did lose Jenny to someone else, and that was also very painful for him. The good news is that he found that he could survive losing. This foundation of growth is what made it possible for Jim to do the right thing with Robin, and establish the relationship with Jenny. Things then played out as they were supposed to, unhampered by his insecurities. *It is much better for a dating relationship to end due to healthy differences than to unhealthy ones.*

In time, Jim went for another woman, Samantha, in whom he was genuinely interested. And this time, he was attracted to her character and values, not her interest in him. Pursuing her was a real risk for him. But in time, Samantha loved him back. They are now happily married. Had Jim not dealt with his past dating approaches, who knows what might have happened instead? The past's examples and warnings (1 Corinthians 10:11) proved a helpful ally for Jim.

Understanding and insight are generally necessary but insufficient elements for breaking free of our pasts. There are times when the truth alone will free us. Most of the time, however, our past patterns point us to some deficits or injuries in our own character makeup. These deficits don't go away unless we enter the process of personal growth.

Be Afraid of Your Past

Another good element of setting boundaries with your dating past is a healthy fear of the consequences of repeating the past. When we clearly understand the prospects we face if things remain the same, it helps us bear the pain of changing. As we have seen, Jim was anxious that he might never marry, or at least not at the age he desired. Jim was able to use his fear to drive the work he needed to do.

Some people believe that Christians should never fear. True, if we are believers, we do not need to fear eternal punishment and separation from God (1 John 4:18). But we do need to live our lives in fear of God because he judges us impartially (1 Peter 1:17). This fear is a healthy concern over our accountability to God for how we conduct our lives. So—be afraid, be very afraid—of the right things. Here are some of them.

Be Afraid of Ruining Your Present Relationship

You may be in a very good relationship right now. But if you have never dealt with your past, you might be endangering this new relationship. Even when you are in a good relationship you will still need to examine your past, find support from God and good friends, and seek wholeness. Doing the hard work of growth now can help prevent problems in the future. Don't neglect your past just because your present is good.

Be Afraid of Staying with Your Present Relationship

Conversely, you may be in a relationship that isn't so good. How would looking at your past help you? Perhaps you will find a dating pattern that demonstrates that you tend to stay even longer in impossible relationships. The sicker it is, the harder you work. Or maybe you realize that you tend to stay with a bad relationship simply because you want to have someone around. Looking at your past may help you to get out of a bad relationship more quickly, thereby saving yourself and your dating partner worlds of hurt.

Be Afraid of Being Injured

Dating relationships matter. People can get inside us into very deep places in our soul. This means that you can invest in and trust someone who is not very trustworthy. Many people who haven't worked on past trust struggles will hope against hope that the next person will be safe, with no ability to guard themselves or discern the trustworthiness of another. The result is often emotional harm. If you look at your past, you will be better able to discern why you were hurt and develop the tools to prevent that hurt in the future.

Be Afraid of Wasting Time

As in Jim's case, most people have some sort of age deadline in their head by which they would like to marry. In reality, you can't wait forever, because you don't have forever. There is such a thing as "too late." So many people who have dreamed all their lives about being married will, in ignoring their pasts, lose their married futures. Get to work on the past!

Be Afraid of Reducing Your Prospects

People who haven't learned lessons from the past are less free to be themselves, grow, and make decisions. This lack of freedom limits their range of choices in the world. For example, say you are drawn to inconsistent, ambivalent men who can't commit. Falling in love with a character problem may ensure that you will not be excited by a stable, available, and accessible man. Your past may label such a man as boring and stodgy, and you risk missing out on an entire segment of potentially rewarding relationships. If you are able to recognize your past dating problems, you will be able to open yourself up to future healthy dating prospects.

Why the Past Still Rules

If there are so many good reasons to work through our past dating patterns, why do people have difficulty in doing so? There are several causes.

Lack of Maturity

One indicator of character maturity is the ability to be aware, curious, and concerned about one's past patterns. The present keeps most of us very busy. It is easy to stay caught up in keeping up with it. However, with maturity comes more ability to

reflect on long-term patterns and issues in life. Remember Jim:
he had dating problems in his twenties. But his immaturity kept
him focused on being busy and enjoying himself. Get into the
spiritual and emotional growth process. In fact, get involved in
the deeper life before you begin noticing significant dating problems. Ask God and safe individuals to help you grow in love
and truth.

Fear of the Unknown

Suppose you found out that you tend to minimize the differences between you and your date, so that there are fewer conflicts. You keep your relationships pleasant, superficial, and
covertly dishonest. You have simply never related to women in
a different way.

As you become aware of your pattern, you may see that your
indirectness is a problem, limiting how close you can be to a
woman. You may want to try to change. However, you are par-
alyzed in your attempts, because you don't have experiences that
give you an indication of what to expect. There are no bad mem-
ories of anyone screaming or crying. But there are no good mem-
ories either. What would happen if you were direct is nothing
but a big question mark. Fearing the unknown—worrying about
what might happen if you change—can stall the growth process.

Which do you prefer: a known bad thing, or an unknown
thing? Many people will choose the known bad thing, as they
have developed ways to live around it and adapt to it. Fearing
the unknown keeps many people from changing who are
painfully aware of their issues. If this is your situation, you
may need to get with close friends and become the honest,
direct person with them that you cannot be with dates. Ask them
for help and reassurance. Work through your fears and defenses
with them. In other words, you need a set of experiences in your
memory to draw on, so that when you apply honesty to the dat-

ing world, you will be comforted in the fact that your unknown thing is now a known good thing. It will help you pursue the relationship in a healthy way.

Fear of the Known

In other cases, some people repeat the past because they have tried to change their patterns and suffered greatly for some reason, not a good one. The pain was sufficient to stop their attempt to change. Taking the above example, suppose you became more direct with your date, and she became offended that you were telling the truth. As a result, she attacked you or left the relationship. This experience, for some people, becomes a template for all future dating relationships with the idea that *if I am honest, bad things happen.*

Actually, this problem is more of a fear of a perceived than an actual unknown. In other words, trying to become more honest should, with healthy people, have good results. People should become closer, more trusting, free, and responsible. But in the above example, it is easy to confuse the problem as being honest, when the problem really is being honest with the wrong person. Be sure you choose people of the light, as there are those who love "darkness instead of light" (John 3:19).

But there are many cases of fears of actual known results also. I know a woman, Linda, who tended to go too quickly into relationships. She would find "the perfect man," become highly committed to him, start making marriage plans, and then would be devastated when he would break up. After her fourth tragedy in two years, she began getting more feedback and support from her friends. As she worked on these issues, she told me one day, "I was afraid of the known problem. At a deep level, I knew these guys wouldn't be long-term prospects. But I was so sad and afraid about being alone, I was willing to put up with them to avoid the alternative." Linda worked very hard on her loneliness-driven overcommitment, and finally began facing and resolving her past within her present relationship support system. As the old Alcoholics Anonymous saying goes, change occurs when the pain of remaining the same is greater than the pain of changing.

Isolation

One major obstacle to resolving the past is the state of being cut off from the source of life, which is relationship with God and others. Many people try to change their patterns all on their own, using willpower, discipline, resolve, and the like. Sooner or later, they tend to fail. A desire to change is generally not enough, or we would have changed before. The Bible teaches that change based simply on willing and choosing is incomplete: "Such regulations indeed have an appearance of wisdom, with their self-imposed worship, their false humility and their harsh treatment of the body, but they lack any value in restraining sensual indulgence" (Colossians 2:23).

Relationship is the fuel which makes change and growth possible. It provides comfort so you can bear the difficulty of change. It creates support for the person as she struggles and fails. It brings reality to her, so that she can change directions and try new ways of solving her problems. If you tend to hide your pain and problems, or if you have difficulty trusting and taking in love, begin working on this with your safe group. You will find that, over time, you have the inner stamina, based on receiving love and support, to deal with the past and resolve it.

A Final Word About the Past

It is important to understand that *you must have a past to resolve it.* In other words, you need to be aware that your past dating patterns have been a problem, and that today you want to change that pattern. Many people are totally unaware that they struggle with their past. And so they repeat the past so much that it is inseparable from the present. In that sense, there is no past, only a continuous, painful present that doesn't work for them. If this is you, ask God to help you begin to repent of (turn from) your pattern today: "If you repent, I will restore you that you may serve me" (Jeremiah 15:19). Repentance creates a break between past and present, so that we may then heal from the effects of the past.

Now that we've looked at the past, we're ready to look at the future. Whom should you be dating? We'll examine that question in the next section.

Take-Away Tips

- With the support and help of God and others, search for the dating patterns of the past which have compromised your relationships.
- Own the patterns instead of assuming that those you have dated are the issue.
- Work on resolving them in the spiritual growth process so that you can choose and act freely in the present in your dating life.
- Develop a healthy fear of not dealing with your past dating patterns.
- Understand and deal with the issues that have kept you from changing your patterns.
- Make a break between past and present with the help of your supportive relationships.

Part Two

Whom Should
I Date?

_____ *Chapter 6* _____

What You Can Live With and What You Can't Live With

_____

*J*n the book *Safe People*, I (Dr. Cloud) told the story of being
asked to speak to a Christian college group on the topic
"How to Pick Someone to Date or Marry." It was a mixed group
and a topic that was certainly on their minds. I opened the talk
with a question: "What do you look for in a person to date seriously or marry?" Here were some of the responses that I got:

- Deep spiritual commitment to God
- A person who loves God's Word
- Someone with ambition
- Someone fun
- Attractive
- Smart
- Witty
- A leader in their field
- Likes sports

"Great list. I like people like that too," I told them. "But let
me share something with you. In all the years that I have done
marriage counseling, I have yet to meet a couple who was ready
to divorce or having significant problems because one was not
witty enough, or did not read their Bible as much as the other

wished, or was not a leader in their field. But I have met hundreds of couples who are about to end their relationship who say things like this:

- She's so controlling that I feel smothered all the time.
- He doesn't listen to me.
- He is so critical. I never feel like I'm doing anything right.
- He is so irresponsible. I never know if the bills have been paid or if he has taken care of the things he promised to do.
- She overspends all the time. She agrees to a budget, and then I get all these bills.
- He can't connect emotionally. He doesn't understand how I feel.
- She is such a perfectionist. I wish she could just accept herself as she is and not be so down on herself all the time.
- His anger scares me.
- I never can believe her after the affair. She lied so much that I have lost all my trust.

I went from there to talk to them about how they composed their own lists of what was important to them and what was not in choosing people to date or get serious with. I told them that there are a lot of differences in tastes that are individual in nature and are fine to have. Some people want athletic people, others want intellectual types. Those differences are what make the world go round and makes dating an interesting time of discovering what you like and don't like. Differences in people's tastes are great.

But there are certain traits that people have which have nothing to do with tastes and natural differences. These are traits which are to be avoided if you are thinking of getting into a serious dating relationship or one which might head toward marriage. These traits have to do with *character*. As I told one young woman, "You are initially attracted to a person's outsides, but over time you will experience his insides. His character is what you will experience long-term and be in relationship with over time."

So, in this chapter, we want you to look at your "boundaries of choices." We want you to look at what your requirements are for the people you date. If you decide and know ahead of time what you will not put up with in a dating relationship, you could save yourself from a season or even a lifetime of misery. On the other hand, you might be too rigid in your preferences and closing yourself off to some good options, and realizing that fact could help you open up to a wider variety of people. There are basically four areas we want you to examine in dating:

1. Some of your preferences might be too limiting, and you need to be more open.
2. Some preferences are more important than you might realize, and you should value them.
3. Some imperfections are minor, and you might have to learn to deal with them.
4. Some imperfections are major, and you should not ever have to live with them. They are totally off limits.

Limiting Preferences

I was talking to a young man the other day about what he was looking for in someone to date or eventually marry. He was making me laugh as he went down his list. He had gotten so particular and perfectionistic that I told him he had basically eliminated the entire market! He wanted his future wife to be a lot of things that were really contradictory and rarely ever seen in the same person, like a hard-driver in business and a stay-at-home mom type. He also had a lot of specific physical requirements that were unrealistic for anyone who did not airbrush themselves daily. I told him he better get ready for a lot of nights alone watching old movies and eating frozen dinners. He did not like what I said.

What about preferences? Shouldn't people have tastes and desires in what they are looking for in people to date? Sure you should. It is all part of knowing who you are and what you like and don't like. But here is our message for you in this area: Know your tastes and what is important to you, but stay open and flexible in dating, for you never know what might happen.

Surprises Happen

"I cannot believe that I married Jason," Sheila said. "It was purely an act of God because he was nothing like I ever thought I would want." Sheila was telling her story to a group at a party. Jason just smiled as he listened to her.

"I was always attracted to the aggressive, sports type who was the up-front kind of guy, always stepping out and seeming like the leader. Jason is nothing like that, initially. He comes across as a lot more reserved. Besides, he was short!

"But a friend told me that she thought I would like him, so we went out. Our first date wasn't that great because I was so closed off to him. But we went out again and I really found myself liking to talk to him. We started to connect, and after a while, I found so many things about him that I had never looked for in a guy. He was such a deep and multifaceted person, that I just could not get enough of him. Pretty soon, I was a goner. I wanted to be with him all the time. I still cannot get enough time with him, and it has been six years! I am so glad that God knew better than I what I wanted. I feel so blessed to be with him."

We have heard examples like that as people opened themselves up to date people who initially didn't seem to be "their type." God showed them that they really did not know what they needed to begin with, and oftentimes that what they thought they wanted would have been bad for them in the end.

Jen was an example like that. She related to me how she had always been afraid to be vulnerable, or "weak and needy" with a guy, so she kept up a very assertive front. A strong business-woman, she impressed a lot of people with this image. But two things were happening as she did this in her dating life. One, she was not bringing her more vulnerable aspects to her male-female relationships, and two, she was attracting passive men. Strong women frequently attract weak men who are looking to be led around.

As she continued to do this, she would get frustrated by the men that she would date as they would be afraid to commit, or would be too passive to ultimately make her very happy. She wanted an equal and was not finding it. But something fortunate happened. She began to grow and find out that her fears of vul-nerability and her softer sides were robbing her in other areas of life, so she began to work through them. As she changed and became more balanced, more balanced men became attracted to her because she had some softness as well. As she put it, "It is a good thing I did not stay like I was. I was always attracted to passive, weak men who could express my own weaker parts for me. That attraction was based on my own problems, not on what was good for me. I need a strong man who can be ten-der, and I would have never been attracted to one until I learned how to be vulnerable and use someone's strength."

As Jen found out, her preference had been based on being unbalanced herself. So you can't always trust preferences to begin with. They can come out in a lot of places that are not so healthy:

- Fears of intimacy can attract you to detached people.
- Fears of autonomy can attract you to controlling people.

- Fears of being real can attract you to perfectionistic people.
- Fears of your own sinfulness can attract you to "bad" people.
- Fears of your own neediness can attract you to weak, passive people.
- Unresolved family of origin issues can attract you to someone who is like a parent that you had trouble with.

And the list goes on. So, the warning here is to observe your preferences and value them, *but be open to the fact that they may not be so good for you after all.* God may know something that you don't know. Be open to getting to know people who are not like you assume you would like, and see what might develop.

In the shallow areas of preferences—like physical shape, personality types, and others—we suggest you be open to casually dating anyone of good character. You might find out a lot about yourself and have a lot of fun. Dating is a time to get to know people and learn. It is a time, in the beginning, of no commitment and exploration. Why say no if the person is of safe character? You might have a good time and learn something as well. We know some people who would not even go out to dinner with anyone who did not fit their list of preferences. That is pretty close-minded. As one woman said, who ultimately found a very good mate, "I would go out with anyone once." She got to see a lot of different types before she decided on one. And she picked well. If they are not dangerous, go out and have a good time!

Important Preferences

On the other hand, some preferences are good to have. You will probably want to have someone who shares (1) common interests, (2) common goals, and (3) common values.

Common Interests

Most strong relationships include at least some common interests. For instance, they both like to hike and backpack, or they both like to minister to teenagers. Common interests allow a couple to spend time together in pursuits they both enjoy. If you live for the outdoors, you probably do not want to get serious with someone who hates going outside and just wants to play with a computer all the time!

Shared interests are very important. People who have little in common will ultimately not spend a lot of time together, or if they do, they won't be doing what they enjoy. You don't have to have all the same interests by any means. But you will probably be better off to have some interests in common. After all, you marry someone to be with them, and what better way to be with them than by doing something together you both love?

Common Goals

Common interests help you determine how you spend your free time. Common goals determine how you spend your life. Your goals will affect where you live, what career you choose, how you spend your time and money, and even how you develop your character and walk with God. Before you get serious with someone, you need to have a good idea of what direction you are going in, and you need to determine whether that person's life is going in the same direction. For example, if you want to be a missionary or inner-city worker living on a limited income, you must share that goal. Or if you are going to pursue graduate school, then you both must share that goal, because it will call for great sacrifices in the relationship.

Interests and goals need to be taken seriously. Not only do they dictate the way that you spend your time and maybe even your life, they also reveal who you really are as a person. If you don't know what interests you, you may use dating to find out—

but don't get serious until you are sure what you like to do! And if you don't know what your goals are, be careful of getting seriously involved with someone. Their goals should not become your goals by default. Know yourself first. Be aware of how differences in interests and goals are going to affect how you spend your time and resources. Don't lie to yourself about interests and goals not mattering to you. They do, and you need to consider the impact that they will have on your relationship.

Common Values

The third area where preferences are important is the area of character. Someone's character is what you are going to experience if you stay in a relationship very long. It is going to be what you abide with, bump into, develop around, share with, receive from, grow with, and so on. If that character is full of good things, then the fruit of your relationship will be good. But if that character is full of thorns and thistles, then you are going to suffer. Believe it. As Jesus said, "a bad tree cannot bear good fruit" (Matthew 7:18). To search for character that shows the fruit of the Spirit—love, patience, kindness, and so forth—would be a good dating goal.

Minor Imperfections You Can Live With

No one is perfect. Every person that you date will be a person who will sin and let you down. There is no Prince Charming that has it all together. So give up that fantasy. However, as you evaluate the people you date, remember a few things.

First, there are sinners that you can live with. Those are people who have the ability to see when they have wronged you, to confess it, to care about how they have hurt you, and to work hard not to continue in that pattern. Anyone who sees where he or she is wrong and tries to change is on the right path and can probably be trusted if that path is not just a momentary turnaround.

If it is truly a path and is continued upon for the long term, that is a good sign. Here are the traits of someone who demonstrates the ability to work on their imperfections:

- A relationship with God
- Ability to see where one is wrong
- Ability to be honest
- Ability to see the effects of the wrong on the other person
- Ability to empathize with those effects and be truly sorry for the other person as opposed to just feeling guilty for themselves
- Motivation to repent and change
- Ability to sustain repentance and change
- Commitment to a path of growth, a system of growth, and the involvement of other people in the growth process
- Ability to receive and utilize forgiveness

If someone can do those things, that is an imperfect person who might be worth betting on. (We also suggest that you work hard at being that person yourself!)

A person of good character will still fail occasionally, but generally they have sins that you can live with. These sins are "yellow lights" in your relationship—things that cannot be ignored, but are not relationship stoppers either. Some patterns can be undeveloped areas of a person's life that are not that bad, and also can be grown out of. They are not lethal, and you can probably live with them, as long as the person sees these problems in him or herself and deals with them in the manner listed above. Here are some examples of things that will annoy you but won't kill you, and you could learn to accept in *mild* doses:

- Disorganization
- Difficulty with opening up and being direct about feelings or hurts

- Tendencies toward performance orientation
- Tendencies towards wanting to appear strong and avoiding vulnerability (often a male disease)
- Perfectionism
- Some attempts to control (like a naturally assertive person being pushy)
- Avoidance of closeness
- Impatience
- Messiness
- Nagging
- Mild forms of other things

We are sure that you could come up with your own list. We all have imperfections, but these flaws will not kill our relationships if we have them in some mild forms. Sometimes, they are not even relationship killers in more significant forms if there is ownership of the problem and the ability to work on it. All of us have ways that we "miss the mark." (That is the Bible's definition of sin.) We all do not get everything right in relationships, and as a result are somewhat of a pain to be with at times. That is normal.

So look at what bothers you. You might be bothered by a normal sinner. You might have not learned how to put up with humanity and be too judgmental or perfectionistic in your demands. Remember, since you have to date sinners, decide which sins you can live with, or at least, work with.

Major Imperfections You Can't (and Shouldn't) Live With

But not all sins are in the yellow category. Some are bright red—as in *stop!* I have often heard people say, "All sin is sin." If by this they mean there is no difference among sins, nothing could be farther from the truth, and that is not what the Bible teaches. It does teach that all sinners are equally guilty before God, and that we all stand in the same state of guilt before him, but not that all sin is equal. Some sins are more damaging than others. As Jesus said clearly, there are "weightier" aspects of God's law, and those are the ones that destroy relationships and hurt people, things like the lack of justice, mercy, and faithfulness (see Matthew 23:23). These sins are inherently destructive, and are more hurtful than the "yellow" sins. (Being messy or impatient with someone can hardly be compared to lying about an affair.)

Lest this stance on sin sound too harsh or nonforgiving, listen to the way that David put it:

> I will be careful to lead a blameless life—when will you come to me? I will walk in my house with blameless heart. I will set before my eyes no vile thing. The deeds of faithless men I hate; they will not cling to me. Men of perverse heart shall be far from me; I will have nothing to do with evil. Whoever slanders his neighbor in secret, him will I put to silence; whoever has haughty eyes and a proud heart, him will I not endure. My eyes will be on the faithful in the land, that they may dwell with me; he whose walk is blameless will minister to me. No one who practices deceit will dwell in my house; no one who speaks falsely will stand in my presence. Every morning I will put to silence all the wicked in the land; I will cut off every evildoer from the city of the LORD. (Psalm 101:2–8)

As David implies in this psalm, <u>character begins with yourself</u>. He decided to avoid:

- Vile things
- Faithlessness
- Perversity
- Evil
- Slander

- Pride and haughtiness
- Deceit
- Wickedness

What an incredible list of character traits to avoid! So many heartaches would be avoided if people would say no to dating someone who showed the above character.

The Bible tells us over and over that some people are worthy of trust and some are not. Jesus himself said, "Do not give dogs what is sacred, do not throw your pearls to pigs. If you do, they may trample them under their feet, and then turn and tear you to pieces" (Matthew 7:6). It is not "unforgiving" to have good boundaries and to not trust a certain kind of person. Staying away from certain people may well protect your heart and life.

We suggest that you have some basic things that you value in your own character, and to require the same from the people that you date. David's list involves these relational and destructive aspects of sin. They are things that hurt people and relationships, and are very harmful. If you encounter such things in a person you are dating, then they are weighty indeed and you should be very, very careful. Listen to them again: faithlessness, perversity, evil, slander, pride, deceit, wickedness. These are certainly red lights and if you encounter them, you should stop right in your tracks and not go further in the relationship until you are certain that the problem is resolved.

But, these are not the only serious issues. In our book *Safe People*, we listed some other traits that are destructive to relationships. Here is the list:

Destructive Personal Traits

- Acts like he has it all together instead of admitting weakness and imperfection
- Is religious instead of spiritual

- Is defensive instead of open to feedback
- Is self-righteous instead of humble
- Apologizes instead of changes
- Avoids working on problems
- Demands trust instead of proving himself trustworthy
- Lies instead of telling the truth
- Is stagnant and not growing
- Is an addict
- Is duplicitous

Destructive Interpersonal Traits

- Avoids closeness
- Thinks only about himself instead of the relationship and the other person
- Is controlling and resists freedom (in dating, this includes not respecting your limits in the physical realm)
- Flatters
- Condemns
- Plays "one up" or acts parental
- Is unstable over time
- Is a negative influence
- Gossips
- Is overly jealous and suspicious
- Negates pain
- Is overly angry

These traits in people are very hurtful character patterns. If they occur infrequently, then maybe you can work through them if your date will take ownership, confess, and work on himself. But if these things are a *pattern*, and there is no ownership, sorrow, and repentance, then watch out. Such patterns can do only two things:

1. Hurt the person on the other end of them.
2. Keep the relationship from being good.

You do not want either one of those. You do not want to be
getting hurt, nor do you want to be dating a person with whom
real relatedness is not possible. If you see these traits, stop where
you are and face them directly. Do not go forward in the relationship without dealing with them. Confront them in the same
manner in which we discussed in chapter 2, "Require and
Embody Truth":

1. Confront the problem directly, stating it in terms of
   your values. "Something that I value in my relationships is acceptance and kindness. When you are critical
   and say mean things about me, I don't like it." Tell him
   that certain things are important to you and that you
   don't want those things violated in your relationships.
2. See what kind of response you get. If the person takes
   ownership, empathizes, apologizes, etc. then that is a
   good sign. Make sure that you are with someone who
   can see when he is wrong and own it.
3. Watch for a pattern of sustained repentance, change,
   and follow-through in growth. It may be necessary to
   take time away if necessary to await true change to
   happen. Don't be afraid of not being with someone
   who has not changed. You do not want the person if
   he is not changing anyway.
4. Only trust again and keep going if these "red lights"
   are no longer problems.

Because of the very nature of human beings, relationships will
be imperfect. You are always going to be dating someone with
flaws. But, remember, there are flaws that you can live with, and
those you can't. The ones that you can live with can teach you
a lot about patience and acceptance, as well as intimacy and
working through conflict. But serious character flaws can destroy

and injure you. The best test is God's Word, and how your own heart feels as you are in a relationship with a person.

If you are dealing with a person who injures you, leaves you feeling bad about yourself and love, and hurts you in other ways, *you are dealing with things that you should not be allowing*. The best test is always your experience of the person. If you are feeling a lot of bad things as a result of being with this person, let that be a sign. The relationship will not get better on its own. Do what you have to do to stop the destruction. Protect yourself by knowing what you feel and value, and have the courage to stick to what you value for your dating life. Ultimately, you will get what you value. Value good things, and say no to things that destroy.

Take-Away Tips

- No human is perfect and you will never have the "ideal" relationship.
- Be open to types and people who are outside your normal tastes and preferences. You never know what you will like until you have gotten to truly know someone.
- Learn the difference between human imperfections that everyone has and are not destructive, just annoying, and character flaws that are seriously damaging to a relationship. Learn to accept the person and deal with the minor problems, and don't allow small things to ruin a relationship.
- Learn what preferences are important to you that you might want to hold onto if a relationship is to be serious. They could affect you for a long time to come.
- Learn what imperfections are not benign, but destructive. They are "red lights" and should be a sign for you that the relationship itself is destructive.

- Learn to take a stand on those issues. Gain the ability to say, like David, that there are certain things you will not tolerate, then stick to your standards. Learn to confront those issues and only trust someone when there is ownership and change.

Chapter 7

Don't Fall in Love with Someone You Wouldn't Be Friends With

Sounds like you and Dennis are becoming an item," I (Dr. Cloud) said to Stephanie. We had tried to get together to catch up for a while, and each time she had been doing something with Dennis.

"No," she replied. "I just like hanging out with him. We enjoy a lot of the same things, and have some wonderful talks. But he's just a friend."

"Why isn't he more?" I asked.

"Oh, I don't know. Whatever that 'thing' is that attracts you to someone—I just don't have it with Dennis. But I do like him a lot and like being his friend."

"I can appreciate that," I said. "Not everyone is meant to fall in love. Do you have the 'thing' you describe happening somewhere?"

"Yeah, I do." I could tell as she said yes that not all was well with whomever the "thing" was with. "His name is Ryan, and I have been dating him about three months. I have the 'thing' with him, that is, I am really attracted to him in the more-than-friends kind of way. But there are some issues."

"What do you mean?" I asked.

"Well, I don't know how to describe it. I am so drawn to him in a physical, romantic kind of way. I get all the butterfly stuff, you know. I think about him a lot and want to be with him. But, after all of that stuff, I don't know what I am doing."

"What do you mean 'you don't know what you are doing'?" I asked.

"Well, there is a lot of romance and that kind of thing. Not that we are sleeping together, but a lot of physicality in the relationship. And I have a lot of 'falling in love feelings.' But there is not a lot more than that when I really look at it. We really don't talk a lot about serious things. It is just this dynamic and longing to be with him that I can't really explain.

"Then there are some things about him that I really would not normally choose. He is not that deep spiritually, and he seems kind of driven in some other ways. And sometimes he really does not communicate. But I know that I am falling for him in some way that I can't describe," she said. "I feel some sort of aliveness when I am with him. There is a deep part of me that he gets to, even though we have kind of a shallow relationship. Doesn't make sense, huh?"

"Sounds like to me that you feel you are 'in love' with Ryan, but have a lot more of a real relationship with Dennis," I observed. "In fact, it sounds like to me that you need to find someone that you have both of those things with. The deep connection and ability to share things that matter, communicate, and have fun like with Dennis, and also the spark and chemistry that you have with Ryan."

"Yeah. That would be nice. But it seems that I always have these two types in my life. There is the kind of guy that I like and the kind I fall in love with. I have never found them together in the same one." She sounded almost weary as she described her dilemma.

I went on to say to Stephanie all that I was thinking at that moment. I knew that I had to for her sake. But I felt for her, in the process, for I knew that she was headed for a heartache. The truth was that she had done this a few times before, and I needed to warn her that she was headed down the same path again. She would let the chemistry that she felt with someone blind her to some very important things that are essential for a good, lasting relationship.

In short, she would fall in love with men that she would not choose as friends. She would go for men who did not share her spiritual commitment, her values, her depth of communication, her interests, and many other aspects of her life. There would just be this attraction that she did not have the ability to justify in any rational sense. The attraction was strong, but unfulfilling, and then she would have to have all her other needs met by a Dennis in her life. Friendship, communication, and good times "just hanging out" were always outside the scope of who she was having romantic feelings for.

A Common Problem

Many singles we've known share Stephanie's problem. Perhaps you do too. You may be attracted to one kind of person, but find that you are better friends with another type, and actually have more of a relationship with the "friend" than the one you are attracted to. In a lot of cases, like Stephanie's, you simply find that the person you are attracted to is not able to connect with all areas of your life. But in other cases it is much more than that. Sometimes you are attracted to someone who is not good for you at all.

You may have all sorts of longings and chemistry with someone who is not only lacking some abilities, but also has some pretty destructive things about her character. She may be self-centered, deceptive in some way, critical, controlling, or ignoring of your needs. You would never choose that kind of person as a friend, because you would have very little in common, and would not want to have to deal with all of her problems. Still, you find yourself desperately attracted to or falling for someone who is just that way. And then, further on in the relationship, the deeper problems will surface and you will find that the relationship has no lasting substance. Nevertheless, even then, you find it difficult to get out of the relationship because you have such a strong attraction to that person.

The Split

One day we were doing a radio show on dating, and a woman called in with the above problem. She said that there were two kinds of men in the world. One was the attractive type that had no character, and the other was the kind with good character and spiritual depth but no attractiveness. "What should I do?" she asked.

"Have you ever thought that there might not really be two types in the world like you have described?" we asked. "But that this might have something to do with you? Maybe you are attracted to shallow or destructive guys for a reason. And maybe you block those feelings of attraction for the good ones?"

"No. It is not that at all. There really are only two types of men in the world. There are the good-looking, strong, attractive ones, and the good guys who are not that exciting. I have seen it over and over," she argued.

"Oh, we believe that you have seen it over and over," we said. "But what we are asking is have you ever considered that this might have something to do with you and not the male race? You might have some sort of split inside of you that is causing you to be drawn to a certain type of man and write off another type."

"No. You guys don't understand. There really are only two types." She went on more adamantly than before.

"So you are telling us that there is not one attractive man that has depth and spiritual qualities about him in the whole world?

And that none of those who do have good depth and character are attractive in any way, shape, or form?" we clarified, just to help her see how foolish she sounded.

"That is exactly right," she said. "I have been dating for a long time and that is exactly what is out there."

"Well, in that case, I guess we will have to see if you are right. Okay, Southern California," we said to our listeners. "We would like all of you singles to drive to our studio right now and get in two lines. If you are attractive in any way, get in one line, and if you have any depth to your character, spiritual life, or personality, get in the other. Then, maybe what we could do is pair you off and get you to help each other out. The ugly, deep ones could disciple the beautiful people, and the beautiful people could give some tips on style, charisma, and other things to the monks and nuns. Then maybe the two groups could become more one and we could get some relationships going here."

It turned out to be an amazing show. We were there for four hours taking calls about this problem. Fortunately, not everyone was as blind to their own responsibility in the issue as the first caller. They could see that there was more to the dynamic than some sort of external explanation like she came up with of there being two types of men in the world. And we had a very stimulating time looking at the things that cause this kind of problem, because it is a very resolvable one, and one that we see people grow out of all the time. We love it when we see a person who has struggled in this area come in and say, "I finally found someone who has all that I have looked for." What a rewarding thing for spiritual and personal growth that is.

Here is what we tell singles who have this problem.

1. If you are attracted to someone who does not possess the character and friendship qualities that you need in a long-term relationship, do not think that you are

going to change him or her. Someone has to go deeper because he or she wants to. <u>Get rid of false hope</u>.

2. See this as a problem. If you see a pattern, do not continue to think that the problem is all external to you, that you just "have not found the right one." We hear so many excuses by people who do not want to see that they have a pattern that they need to examine regarding the way that they see people, or the people they attract, or the ones that they are attracted to.

3. Do everything possible to make yourself aware of the reality of the person you are drawn to and the relationship that you have. Ask yourself:

   • Do you feel like all of your parts are being related to?
   • Can you share all of your values?
   • Is the spiritual commitment the same?
   • Are there character traits that you find yourself ignoring, denying, or excusing?
   • In short, *would you pick this person as a friend?*

   Then make sure that you talk to someone else about these issues. Denial is more difficult to maintain if you are talking to someone and confessing what is true.

4. Are you confusing longing for "being in love"? Many times people long for a certain kind of fantasy person and confuse this deep longing as being in love. Remember, love satisfies. It does not leave you romantically pining.

5. Are you confusing infatuation with love? Infatuation is a projection of needs and idealized fantasies onto a person that have little to do with who that person really is. Many times people come up with a kind of person who symbolizes a lot of things that they need or idealize and feel that they are falling in love with

someone when in reality it is a fantasy that will not last. Remember the phrase "in fat you ate." Infatuation is very similar to high-fat fast food. No lasting nutritional value!

6. Above all, find an accountability system to hold you to the boundary of not letting yourself go too far into a relationship with someone that you would not be friends with. *Say no to letting your heart get involved with a person whom you would not choose as a friend.*

Resolving the Split

This is not a book on working through all of the kinds of issues that will cause you to be attracted to the wrong kind of person. Our book *Safe People: How to Find Relationships That Are Good For You and Avoid Those That Aren't* was written to help with that issue, and also our books *Changes That Heal* and *Hiding from Love*. The main point here is that you need to have some good boundaries with yourself in terms of allowing yourself to get further into relationships with someone you would not want to be friends with.

However, here are a few reasons that you may be attracted to the wrong kind of person.

Unresolved Family-of-Origin Issues

If you had problems in the family you grew up in, those problems may surface in your dating relationships. For example, you may be attracted to a person who is like a parent you struggled with. One woman I know had a father who was extremely critical. As she grew up, she continually struggled to gain his approval but never received it. As a result, she was desperately attracted to critical men that she could never please. She would never have wanted friends like that, but she would "fall in love" with men who had that kind of character.

Or you may be attracted to someone who is the diametrical opposite of your hurtful parent. I know another woman who had such an aggressive father that she feared any kind of strength and drive in a man. As a result she would always be attracted to very passive, loving men, but they would always frustrate her because they could not stand on their own two feet.

In both cases, neither woman had resolved her original problem with an old relationship, and as a result they were trying to resolve them through present relationships. This never works. Deal with each relationship on its own merit so that it will not interfere with others.

Unintegrated Parts of Yourself

Another prime reason you may be attracted to people who would not be good for you is that you are looking to resolve some aspect of yourself that you have never faced. Sometimes it is a good thing, like assertiveness. I know one man who had never integrated his own sense of assertiveness and strength and was always attracted to women who were domineering and controlling because he was drawn to the strength that he could not possess on his own. Often if you do not possess a certain quality, you are drawn to someone who possesses it in the extreme. In other words, a passive person will not be drawn to someone who is normally assertive, but someone who is equally split in the opposite direction—someone who is overly domineering.

Sometimes you may be attracted to a bad thing. If you have always been the "good" person, you may be drawn to someone who embodies some sort of "dark" side. The dark side could be sexual, substance abuse, irresponsibility, or impulsivity, but whatever it is, the "saint" falls head over heels with the "sinner." This explains the heartache of many parents of adolescent girls! The good girl from the good family falls for the "bad boy."

This common pattern occurs when you are not able to look at and integrate your own "badness." You may feel ashamed that you are not perfect, and you don't want to face some of the aspects of your own soul that need to be addressed. Because of either external or internal demands that you be "good," you don't open up and integrate the "shadow" sides of yourself and turn into a real person. You have a good-bad split inside that shows up by your being good but being attracted to the bad. The resolution for this is to become neither "good" nor "bad," in a split way, but *real*, with both good and bad parts. (See Luke 11:39–40; Ecclesiastes 7:16–18.) If you can find safe, healing relationships to integrate the parts of yourself you are ashamed of, you won't be drawn to darkness on the outside.

Sometimes you may have a pain or hurt that you have never faced. Someone with unresolved hurt can be attracted to a person with a lot of pain and problems as a way of connecting with his own angst. This is the classic codependent syndrome.

Whatever the issue, there are countless people who have denied parts of themselves and are drawn to problematic situations as an attempt to work out those issues. As Proverbs 4:23 says: "Above all else, guard your heart, for it is the wellspring of life." Whatever is in your heart is what you are going to find yourself dealing with, in one way or another. Guard your heart and make it healthy so you will not be attracted to the wrong kinds of people.

Defensive Hope

Have you had a lot of disappointment and loss in your life? If so, it may be difficult for you to let go of things, even things that are not good. You may have unknowingly developed a character pattern of "defensive hope." You hope for things to change as a defense against the loss of letting them go, for the grief of letting go would be overwhelming to you. Seeing that a person is not going to be what you need long term, you will hang on to hope for change instead of going through the pain of loss.

Romanticizing

Do you describe yourself as a "hopeless romantic"? If so, you may be vulnerable to charmers, who can draw you in to romantic kinds of dynamics, but without the underlying character to carry on a lasting relationship. As the Bible says, "Charm is deceptive" (Proverbs 31:30). Charmers and their prey are unable to get past romanticization to real intimacy. Many sexual or romance addicts fall into this category. The romantic drama and sexual energy of the relationship distract them from the underlying emptiness of a relationship that's devoid of intimacy. As one woman told me, "We were taking our emptiness to the bedroom and mutually denying it."

If you have a tendency to romanticize, then you might have a tendency to live in a world of fantasized relationship. This is sometimes fine in the beginning of a relationship, for a season, and in a limited way. Fantasy is often what some of attraction consists of. But if a relationship cannot go past fantasy into sustained intimacy and real connection, the whole thing is a sham and your emptiness must be faced.

We are not saying that romance, sexuality, and passion are bad. On the contrary, they are absolutely essential. If you spend a lot of time with a growing relationship and never feel any passion or sexual attraction, then either something is wrong or this person really is someone that you should keep in the "friend" category. Sexuality and intimacy must come together for a relationship to be deep and fulfilling. Sex is part of God's design for erotic love in marriage and must be developed as well as platonic love, connectedness, and friendship. But passion without character, intimacy, and friendship to undergird it is extremely dangerous.

If you are a romantic, you may have a longstanding Cinderella complex. Or your fantasies may be a defense against depression or other kinds of disappointments. But, as wonderful as romance is, if it is not based on the reality of someone's character, it is going to be heartbreaking in the end. If you are a romantic by style or necessity, keep the good aspect of that, but work through the ways that it may be keeping you from facing some realities. The old "wining and dining" dynamic that lures people in is not a long-term basis for relationship. Friendship is.

In fact, the better path is where real connection and friendship is the beginning and romance grows from that. More about that later, but for now, remember that if you have a tendency to romanticize everything, then you are avoiding the reality of what is going on. And the reality is what you are going to have to live with.

Undeveloped Intimacy

Some people have not ever been connected with and known at a very deep level. At their most vulnerable parts of their heart, they have never been related to. So, they don't really know what real connection and intimacy is. They might have come from a disconnected family or church background. Whatever the case, they don't even know what they are missing.

If this is your experience, you will likely be drawn to people who cannot connect either. Detachment often is drawn to detachment, for reasons of familiarity as well as the safety of remaining unknown. It is as if you say to your date, "You seem to be the same as me. Let's be disconnected together." Or you just do not know better. But the end result is that you are attracted to a disconnected character and "fall in love" as the fantasy life takes over from the disconnected part of yourself.

The cure for disconnection is to make sure that you are in healing relationships that are not romantic in nature so that all of your parts can be related to and find connection. Then you will have developed the capacity for intimacy and being known at all levels, and you will choose people who can know you at those levels as well.

Friendship Is the Path

Romance is great. Sexuality is great. Attraction is great. But here is the key: *If all of those are not built upon lasting friendship and respect for the person's character, something is wrong.*

A real and lasting relationship must be built upon friendship first. You are going to spend a lot of time with that person. As one friend of mine said about picking her mate: "He was someone I knew I could grow old with. I liked spending time with him. And he made me laugh." She also shared deep spiritual values and other commonalties with him as well, as she would with any other friend. They have been married for nearly thirty years.

The best boundary that you can have in your dating life is to begin every relationship with an eye toward friendship. Do not rush into any kind of romance. Keep your boundaries, physically, emotionally, and otherwise. Spend time with a person. Spend time getting to know them in nonromantic ways. Spend time with that person in groups of other friends. How well does he or she fit in? How well do you fit in with his or her friends? Does he or she even have friends? (If they do not have long-term friendships, that is a bad sign.)

If you do not allow yourself to rush into falling for someone that you have not become friends with first, you will be more sure when you let yourself go to the next step. Certainly you might find yourself having all sorts of feelings. Enjoy them. *But do not believe them.* Only believe your experience of getting to know a person and seeing if you can share at a deep level. See if you find that he or she is a person of the kind of character you would trust as a friend. And as important as all of that, *see if that person is a person that you would like spending time with if there were no romance at all.* That is the one true measure of a friend, a person with whom you like to spend time, having no regard to how you are spending it. "Hanging out" is fulfilling in and of itself. And that, long-term, requires character, and in the deepest of friendships, shared values as well. You would want your best friends to be honest, faithful, deep, spiritual, responsible, connecting, growing, loving, and the like. Make sure that those qualities are also present in the person you are falling in love with.

Keep your boundaries. We guarantee that being lovers with someone you would not want to be friends with is no good thing at all.

Take-Away Tips

- If you find that you are not really friends with someone you have a "crush" on, let that be a warning signal that something is wrong.
- Do not think that someone who has no character is going to develop it just because you want him or her to grow.
- If being attracted to the wrong person is a pattern, do not blame it on external reasons, but take responsibility for being the one who has a problem and work on finding its cause.
- Make yourself face the hard questions about the person you are with. With the help of friends, be honest about whether or not you really "like" the person as well as have "chemistry" with him or her. Romantic feelings can be very deceptive, and even pathological. They are not "true love."

- Friendship and shared values are the things that last in a relationship. Do not believe your romantic feelings.
- Romance is great. Sexuality is great. Attraction is great. But here is the key: If all of those are not built upon lasting friendship and respect of that person's character, something is wrong.
- Friendship should always be an underlying foundation of any romantic relationship. Romance is fleeting, and comes and goes. Friendship lasts. Both are important in a lasting relationship.

——— *Chapter 8* ———

Don't Ruin a Friendship
Out of Loneliness

Recently, I (Dr. Townsend) attended a friend's wedding. Ellen had wanted to marry for a long time, and God brought Jeff and her together in a meaningful way. The wedding celebrated the union of a couple that truly seemed right for each other. During the reception, several toasts were made. One was from Ted, who has been best friends with Ellen since junior high school. He congratulated the couple and wished them the best. At the same time, it was obvious that he had some sadness also. He was still single, and experienced some pangs of loss that his relationship with Ellen was going to have to change somewhat. She would not be as available to Ted as she had been before she married Jeff, a reality that they both accepted as being a good thing. Yet it was still painful for Ted.

I have known these two friends for a long time, and I empathized with Ted. I remembered that over the years they knew each other, they seemed so compatible and happy together. Several people had suggested, "You two are really right for each other. Why don't you date?" Finally they did try to date. But for both of them, the experience was like, as the saying goes, "Kissing your sister (or brother)." The romantic part of the connection simply did not exist. That sort of closeness even seemed to confuse the friendship feelings that they had had for each other.

So the two figured that they were a safe harbor for each other, and kept things platonic. The relationship was very satisfying and fulfilling for both. Each had an opposite-sex friend who gave them the unique support and perspective which same-sex friends can't provide.

Ted and Ellen's friendship is an example of two things. First, it illustrates how much good can come from healthy opposite-sex relationships. And second, it shows how much grief they spared themselves by not pursuing a romantic relationship when the feelings were simply not there. And that is the topic of this chapter: helping you experience the good that comes from friendships and avoid the problems that come from making friendships into something they are not.

Romanticizing a Friendship

Romantic feelings come from an idealization of the other person. In our heads, we believe our beloved is perfect and experience all sorts of strong feelings, such as intense longings to be with him, admiration, and sexual desire. This idealization can be caused by several things, both healthy and unhealthy:

1. In a new relationship, you don't know much about the other person. Idealization fills in the gaps with good things in order to keep the couple involved in the relationship, and helps them tolerate the early parts of the developing connection.

2. In a mature relationship, romantic idealization waxes and wanes through the connection at various times. It arises out of a deep appreciation and gratitude for the person's presence and love, yet it retains the reality of who he is at the same time.

3. In a struggling relationship, one person can develop romantic feelings for the other out of his own neediness. This neediness becomes "romanticized," that is, it disguises its true nature in romance. The person feels alive, driven, and motivated to be with the other. Yet the need is generally caused by some emptiness inside.

It is this third cause that can ruin a perfectly good friendship. How do dependent feelings turn into romantic ones? Romanticization occurs when a lonely person is unable to safely feel and act appropriately upon his lonely emotions. Actually, loneliness is a good thing, in and of itself. It is a signal that we need something from the outside, be it comfort, support, or empathy. It keeps us from starving emotionally. God has designed us to respond to that signal. If you are hungry, go get a burger. If you are lonely, go get plugged into a relationship. It is not all that simple, but that is the essential idea.

However, many people have difficulty here. For some reason or another, their God-given need for relationship becomes distorted into something that makes them and their friends pretty miserable. They may have a history of attempting to turn friendships into something more. Or they may have this happen only once or twice in life. The words that cut them the deepest are the kindly intended "I really like you—as a friend."

Actually, there are two types of loneliness. The first is the type that indicates that we need to be in day-to-day contact with others. Relationship is an ongoing process. We need pretty constant refills of support and presence from others to keep us going. For example, a salesman who goes off on a long business trip feels lonely for his support network while on the road, and takes steps to reconnect when he returns.

A second type describes a problem condition. This type of loneliness is a chronic, longstanding sense of emptiness in life, no matter what the circumstances. The person can be around many loving, caring people, and still feel isolated. She may either feel that others don't care, or that she is unable to receive what they give. This loneliness is an indication that something is broken in one's soul, and needs to be repaired in God's healing process.

Whatever type of loneliness people experience, there are several causes of romanticization.

Conflicts in Experiencing Dependency

People who romanticize often are unable to feel their dependency for what it is: dependency. Dependency is actually a blessed state: "Blessed are those who hunger and thirst for righteousness, for they will be filled" (Matthew 5:6). That is a good thing, for when we respond to it, God fills us up with the good things we need. Yet many people's dependent feelings are cut off. They are unable to experience loneliness *as loneliness*, emptiness *as emptiness*, relational hunger *as relational hunger*. There is good reason for this. While loneliness is a good, God-given emotion, it is not always a pleasant one. It indicates a state of deprivation, need, and incompleteness. Feeling deprived can be very painful. And we often try to deny what is painful, in order to stay away from the feeling.

Here are some reasons people are unable to feel their hunger:

- They may fear the depth of their internal emptiness.
- They may feel badness associated with loneliness. People who have had angry and detached relationships often have intense feelings of badness.
- They may feel ashamed of being needy.
- They may be afraid to risk reaching out for fear of being hurt.
- They may feel helpless and powerless when they feel their needs.

As a result, lonely people may not feel like lonely people should, which is lonely. However, they may feel other things instead, such as irritation, depression, addictive drives, and romantic cravings. These are often far more acceptable and tolerable. The problem is, however, that acting on these "false" feelings does not meet the real needs for compassion, care, and comfort. If you have ever had an addiction, or dated someone with one, you understand how the substance often slakes some desires, but actually helps keep the person disconnected from the life of relationship.

Still other people may be able to experience their loneliness, but they are in conflict with it. They don't deny their loneliness, but they certainly don't see it as a good thing. Their neediness is painful and unpleasant. So they don't act on it. For example, a friend of mine once told me, "I date women that I'm not really excited about, so that I don't have to take a risk. I just hate that sense of wanting someone who might not want me."

Failures in Relating to the Same Sex

Often, those who romanticize their friends have a history of not being able to safely and deeply connect to the same sex. They may feel many negative things about those of the same sex:

- Worried that they will hurt the other person
- Doubt that they have anything to offer
- Contempt for the stereotypical weaknesses of their gender
- Fear that they will lose opposite-sex opportunities by spending time with same-sex friendships

Yet they may feel just the opposite with opposite-sex relationships. They will feel energized, charged up, and alive after a good romantic encounter. Often, these people have experienced problems in the past with same-sex relationships. For example, a woman may have had a distant, controlling, or enmeshing mother and therefore overconnected to her father to get her needs met. Or she may have had a seductive father who attempted to get in between her and her mother's connection. Whatever the cause, the dependency needs that should be met in healthy same-sex ways are being acted out in the romantic sphere.

Romantic feelings are ultimately for adults. They are a way to prepare us for one of the most adult processes in life, which is marriage. The needs that romanticizers have are pre-adult needs, such as for belonging, being safe, and feeling comforted and loved. These needs are to be met primarily with God and your safe nonromantic relationships. Keep these relationships a major part of your life. It will help you go for romance from a full adult perspective, not that of a lonely child.

If you have had a friend with this struggle, you may have noticed that you are sort of a "bus stop" for him. When he is in between girlfriends, he wants to spend all sorts of time with you. But when he finds someone, you don't hear from him for a long time. You're on the bus stop bench, and he's just hopped the romanticizing bus for another tour.

Idealizing Romance

Related to this is the problem of thinking that romance is the highest form of friendship. Many people who are "into" romance (watch out for anyone who tells you that!) feel that friendship is a grade lower than a romance. Thus, they will attempt to develop romantic feelings with someone that they are friends with, believing they are taking the friendship to a better and deeper level. I had a friend tell me that she did this several times with high school and college friends. They thought, *We're so close, there must be romance here.* Luckily, as she related to me, "We backed off, even though at the time we thought we were missing the higher road. Now, in our thirties, we are married to other people. And we are all glad about it."

Romantic relationships are not better than friendships. They are different and meet different needs. Do not get caught in the idea that you are missing out by keeping your friend as "only" your friend.

Rescue/Caretaking Roles

Sometimes, people who get caught up in romanticizing have tendencies to get into certain ways of relating called *rescuing* and *caretaking*. The "rescuee" will signal a need for someone to take care of him. The "caretaker" will receive the signal and go support, comfort, or solve the problems of the rescuee. This sort of relationship has to do with people's struggles in directly taking responsibility for their lives, or in being able to receive, rather than give.

This sort of pattern becomes easily romanticized on both sides. The rescuee asks for a parent to protect him, and falls in love with that parent. The caretaker looks for someone to fix, and then falls in love with the grateful child. You see rescuing and caretaking played out in many ways in the world of dating:

- The man who has been wounded by so many women
- The woman who believes that her love can repair that hurt man
- The woman who can't get her finances and career together
- The man who thinks he can get her on her feet

If you play this game, one of you is taking a child role. And while it may feel warm and loving now, remember that children one day grow up. They will struggle for their freedom and autonomy. It is not pleasant to be married to someone who thinks you are their controlling parent.

Impulsiveness

Some people struggle with romanticization because they have difficulty with their drives and impulses. They become sexually intimate (an oxymoron) very quickly, or are into quick, intense, "deep" connections. They thirst for the experience of romance, as it makes them feel vibrant and alive. A friendship feels like vanilla pudding, but in a romance they can let out all sorts of loving and aggressive feelings and behaviors. It is as if romance is the place they can let it all hang out.

The problem here is that impulses are to be matured and structured in healthy ways, not simply acted on when they tell us to. That is the essence of self-control. Impulsive romanticization is an ineffective shortcut to the truly higher road of deep, satisfying relationships. Learn to verbalize, express, and deal with your strong impulses in ways that bring healthy connection, not a history of intense and broken connections.

How Can I Know If This Is a Friendship or a Romance?

But how can you tell if your present relationship is the real thing, or is one you have created to keep you out of your loneliness? Do you have to "kiss your sister" with every friendship to test it out? These are important questions, whether you are on the curative or preventive end of things. Here are some ways to see if you are wrecking a friendship by romanticizing.

Get Connected Outside of the Relationship

We all need people who will love us, support us, and tell us the truth on a continual basis. This provides an emotional foundation that helps keep relationships in perspective for what they truly are. So many people we have asked about their dating tragedies have told us, "I have always been lonely, and moved too fast" or "I had just gotten out of a bad marriage and was so alone." The need to be connected with others cannot be overemphasized. In fact, it is almost impossible for you to follow the remaining suggestions here until you are first connected to others, because your deep needs for relationship can distort your thinking and objectivity. So drop this book for a week and start finding some safe places where you can also relate without a date!

Evaluate the Fruits of the Relationship

What do you value in the relationship? True romance and romanticization are after very different goals. Here is a table that will help you find out:

Healthy Romance	Romanticized Friendship
Desire is based on first being rooted in love elsewhere.	Desire is based on empty neediness for the other person.
Other's freedom is valued.	Other's freedom is a problem.
Relationship draws in friends.	Relationship shuts others out.
Conflicts work out okay.	Conflicts threaten the relationship.
Mutual feelings.	One person feels romantic, the other doesn't.
Friendship and romantic feelings coexist.	All-friend or all-romantic feelings; can't be both at the same time.

As you can see, sooner or later romanticization should break down the relationship if you are engaging in it unawares. A romanticized friendship will not meet the needs that romantic love should meet. It is a very good thing to find that out before marriage.

Get Feedback

Ask your friends if you are a romance addict. If they have ever sat on the bus-stop bench waiting for you between relationships, or if they have ever felt used or neglected by you, they may have a good answer for you. Ask them to evaluate you as a friend. Ask if they know the deeper parts of who you are. Find out where you are emotionally invested in the lives of others.

If You Are on the Receiving End . . .

Natalie and Spencer had been dating several months. She had been very attracted to his friendliness, fun attitude, and values. Spencer had recently come off of a painful breakup with a girlfriend. At first, Natalie had been concerned about a rebound effect. However, he seemed to be so into the relationship that she stopped worrying. They were having a great time.

Recently, Natalie had begun worrying again. Spencer seemed to want more time and commitment than she was ready to give. He wanted to know where she was all the time. Worse, when they were together, all he wanted to do was cling to her and have her listen to him complain about his problems. She felt more like a mom than a woman who was being pursued by a man. They dated several more months like this, because Natalie didn't want to hurt Spencer; she often enjoyed the relationship, and he helped her own loneliness.

Finally, they started talking about her feelings. It turned out that Natalie had reason to be concerned. Spencer owned up to the problem. He told her, "I just need someone to care about. When I don't have that special person, I can't stand the emptiness." Natalie was relieved, as she was able to understand her experience better. The relationship ultimately did not last. However, Spencer subsequently got into a support group to help him resolve his dependency, rather than going to another serial relationship. And Natalie found someone who wanted a companion, not a parent.

If you identify with Natalie's experience, it helps to see yourself as part of the problem. Natalie enjoyed Spencer's presence. However, she waited a long time to admit to herself that she was dating a lonely man with whom she would have been better off in a friendship. She did this because she enjoyed his attentiveness, she didn't want to hurt him, and because *she was also a lonely person.*

You may find yourself in the same boat. You are doing yourself and your date no favors by avoiding the reality. Early childhood feelings and parts of ourselves will ultimately cause some problems in a grown-up dating relationship, if they have no other relationships in which to be healed and matured. Pay attention to things like openness, freedom, mutuality, and the like. If you avoid the issues, you can keep a lonely person from ever dealing with a problem that God wants to help him with, and you can waste a lot of your time and energy. Be part of the solution for both of you.

Take-Away Tips

- Explore your loneliness to see if it is the normal need for connectedness, or a sign of an injury that needs to be healed.
- Be aware that romantic feelings, though a good thing, can disguise deep loneliness and confuse how you pick people.
- Become deeply involved in your friendships, and value the good things you're getting out of them; this can fulfill you inside and help resolve the tendency to romanticize platonic relationships.

- Don't be afraid of dependent feelings. Use them to seek out good people.
- Stay in touch with safe and truthful friends who can help you see when you create something in a relationship that isn't there.

Chapter 9

Beware When Opposites Attract

_____

*H*e is so strong and I'm so insecure."

"She's a people person and I'm into my own space."

"He's good at making money and I'm good at spending it."

"She is confident and I need reassurance."

"He's everything I'm not. He completes me."

Completion. At our deepest part, we all want and need it. To be complete is to become whole, without deficit, or undivided. At some level, most of us are aware that we do not possess completion, that we are unfinished and not what we should be. Yet there is within us a God-given desire to find the missing pieces that will finish us. This desire drives us toward relationships and experiences that will help us attain completion. Yet, as we will see, this desire can also be confused with the desires of dating and mating, and bad things can happen.

This is the problem of the "opposites attract" mentality. The thinking is that you bring to the table certain qualities, and your date brings the opposite qualities. The result of your relationship is that you both end up better off; the sum is greater than the parts. For example, you may be a careful but sometimes indecisive person. You fall in love with a guy who knows what he wants and goes for it. You may think, *What a good fit! He can help me learn to know what I want and go after it!*

Differing Gifts Are Good for Relationships

Indeed, there is a lot of value in people bringing strengths to a relationship, as no one is Superman. Our lives are always enriched by being connected to others who have abilities we don't have. Any businessperson will tell you that job descriptions and training are quite individual. You want your analytical, detail-oriented people in accounting, and your creative, brainstorming people in marketing.

The same is true in the church. The Bible teaches that we all have different gifts, or abilities, that we bring to our relationships and the world: "There are different kinds of gifts, but the same Spirit" (1 Corinthians 12:4). Some are more talented in administration, while others bring teaching abilities to the body of Christ. No believer is self-sufficient.

The idea of complementary gifts and strengths is good for us emotionally, in more than one way. We have to learn humility to ask people for what we don't possess, and that helps us grow. For example, if your date is perceptive in relationships, you might ask him why you are struggling in your relationship with your roommate. In addition, we also can grow from the competencies of others. When my son Ricky wanted to sign up for organized basketball, I wanted to help coach him, but I didn't know much about the sport. So I called Dan, a friend who knows the game, and whose son Zack is a friend of Ricky's. We decided to co-coach a team that included our sons, with Dan as head coach and me as assistant. Though I am not gifted in the way Dan is in basketball, I learned so much about the sport that season. So we are enriched and helped by taking advantage of the differing gifts of others.

The Problem of Opposite Attractions

We should use and appreciate the abilities of those who have what we don't. However, the danger occurs when *we make opposing styles or abilities a basis for relationship.* At the outset of the relationship, this may seem like a good thing. You are complementing each other. You each provide what the other needs. You are stimulated by the other's different point of view.

However, the danger of going for an opposite-type person is this: *opposite-driven relationships often confuse dependency with true love.* That is, people may feel intense longings and attractions for an "opposite" person. They may appreciate the "completion" they feel with that person. But they run the risk of simply needing that person for those functions, and never giving the true loving feelings any relationship needs to grow and flourish. Dependency is only part of love. It is not the full expression of love. The full expression of love is to give back from a full heart.

For example, Lindsey was more of a lover than a fighter. She was good at caring and connecting with others, but she had a hard time with assertiveness and conflict. It seemed she often ended up having to put up with maltreatment or inconsiderateness from others. She was a nice person, and therefore a magnet for irresponsible persons.

Lindsey started dating Alex, who was her opposite in this area. Alex was strong, confident, and had no problems entering into conflict for what he believed was right. He had clear moral and spiritual values, was successful in his career, and took initiative to solve his problems. Lindsey was attracted to Alex's strength. She was even more smitten when it helped her own life. For example, Lindsey's apartment manager neglected to have an electrical wiring problem repaired after she had made several requests. She mentioned the problem to Alex over dinner. The next day, he had called her manager. Lindsey never found out what he said to him, but the wiring was fixed within twenty-four hours. She was elated, grateful, and even more attracted to Alex. He certainly had other good qualities, such as being caring, responsible, and funny. But she felt a lot of relief when she encountered conflicts that Alex would handle for her.

The relationship continued to grow and deepen. However, Lindsey began relying more and more on Alex to enter into conflict that she felt ill-equipped to deal with. He negotiated with her garage mechanic over problems with her car. He talked to her boss about her weekend work hours. He even confronted her mother on how she used guilt to get Lindsey to make inopportune visits.

Finally, the confrontational Alex sat Lindsey down for their own confrontation. He explained, "I really love you, but I'm starting to feel some resentment. I don't mind helping you; it makes me feel useful. But with some of these relationships you are afraid of dealing with, I'm feeling more used than useful."

Lindsey understood what Alex was saying. She had been utilizing the "opposite-thinking" mentality to keep from working on her own growth—specifically, her fear of conflict, anger, and arguments. She agreed that she had been using Alex without realizing it, and she began working on assertiveness in her support group at church. She told him, "Let me know the next time I ask you to do my dirty work for me." Alex appreciated her attitude.

This story ends well, as the two eventually married and are happy together. But the problem could have resolved in very different ways:

- Alex could have quietly resented Lindsey, and the relationship could have disintegrated.
- Lindsey could have disagreed with Alex, thinking it was his job in the relationship to solve these problems.

- Alex could have used his confrontation abilities to control and manipulate her in the relationship.
- Lindsey could have despaired at her inability to stand up for herself.
- Lindsey could have resented Alex's abilities, and seen him as domineering instead of working on becoming more assertive herself.

Had Lindsey not been a growing-type person, she may have remained conflict-avoidant, always looking to Alex to do that which she was afraid or unwilling to do.

Why Opposites Attract

The phrase "opposites attract" does have some truth to it. Opposites are drawn to each other, in many styles:

- Extroverts and introverts
- Analytic and visionary
- High energy and laid-back
- Thinking and feeling
- Disciplined and spontaneous
- Relationship-seeking and shy
- Confident and insecure
- Self-absorbed and giving
- Critical and accepting

What is it about opposites that people find so attractive? Why are we attracted to our opposite? There are several answers to this question.

We Do Not Want to Work at Developing Ourselves

Often, we date and want "opposite" people because we do not want to do the work of developing for ourselves what the other person does well. Whatever her opposite trait is, it appears easier to appreciate, admire, and use hers rather than to grow in that area. It is a matter of not taking ownership of what we need to repair or develop in our character.

In the above example, Lindsey initially was happy to let Alex do her confronting for her. She felt safe, relieved, and protected. She hadn't realized yet that she was neglecting an area of growth that she needed to work on. *And that is the essence of the opposite issue. It is not really about the other person. It is about using another person to avoid dealing with our own souls.* When we decide to stop piggybacking on someone else's strengths, they are not the problem. We are. And growth can begin.

We Want to Be Complete

One reason people are initially drawn to an individual with opposite traits is a pretty healthy one. It is that *we are drawn to those who possess what we do not, so that we can internalize and own that trait for ourselves.* This is a good thing, as that is how God designed the growth process. We are to receive training in life from others, then pass our knowledge and abilities down to others over the generations, for their own benefit.

Therefore, suppose you are a type-A person who is dating an emotionally driven person. You might be attracted to his feeling responses to life because it is a part of growth that you want to develop in yourself. He is more developed in that area than you, and so may have something to offer. This is a good thing.

Though this really is how we grow, dating is not a good arena in which to develop oneself in a specific and important aspect of growth. Though your date may be a good supportive example, he is still a date, not a mentor, teacher, or counselor to you. Also, since dating is not a permanent commitment, you run a risk that you will lose that person's benefits to you. It is much better to go to non-dating relationships in order to mature and grow with the tutelage of others who have what you are working on possessing.

We Are Afraid of Dealing with Our Deficits

Another reason that opposites attract is our fear of looking at our own character flaws. Self-exploration and change can be scary. We may be afraid of dealing with our inability or weakness, in several aspects:

- Making mistakes and failing
- Risking making others angry
- Having others leave us
- Guilt over hurting others
- Re-experiencing a painful past
- Looking at parts of ourselves that we don't like to see

Lindsey's issue with Alex was fear-based. She was not an irresponsible person, but she had come from a family in which being polite, nice, and compliant were seen as virtues, while honesty, confrontation, and limit-setting were seen as selfish sins. She had grown up believing that telling the truth was hurtful, and she hated conflict. So she was terrified of dealing with problems with people.

We Are Spiritually Lazy

Irresponsibility is the other side of the coin. It is simply easier to have others do for us what we don't want to do for ourselves. This is the nature of immaturity, or "spiritual laziness." Actually, life does begin with others doing for us. Infants are dependent on mothers to do virtually everything. Babies have very little of what they need to survive inside of them. They learn how to take in from the outside that which they don't possess. The Bible illustrates this process: "Like newborn babies, crave pure spiritual milk, so that by it you may grow up in your salvation" (1 Peter 2:2).

But this isn't irresponsible behavior for an infant, it is his task. God designed him so that as he takes in love, support, safety, care, instruction, and discipline, he internalizes these things and develops them for himself. What was once outside of us now becomes part of us. Immaturity, however, is when a person fails to take ownership for what he has internalized, and continues to demand that others provide it for him. The rageaholic has to have his girlfriend soothe him when he is angry, rather than learning to self-soothe and deal with his rage. The impulsive Nordstrom's shopper depends on her boyfriend to sort out her tangled finances. The introverted man looks to his girlfriend to maintain the relationships he should be developing. This is not appreciating someone's strengths. Instead, one person is not taking stewardship of his life, and the other is taking too much stewardship of that same life.

So whether the problem be fear or laziness, we need to deal with our own deficits instead of looking to a date to heal them.

We Rely on Our Partner's Gifts Rather Than Dealing with Our Character Deficits

Sometimes the problem can be a confusion between giftedness and character deficits. A woman may think her boyfriend is simply more gifted in decision-making and finances than she is, and hands over that part of her life to him. Though he may be more gifted, competent, or trained, that is not the issue. We are all to carry our own load in life. While we are to go to others for help in areas, we are still to take ownership of our lives. If you find yourself continually needing to go to your date for things you should be doing for yourself, you may be confusing giftedness with character issues.

What would a dating relationship look like in which giftedness and ability were appreciated, but the two people were still taking ownership of their lives? There are a few indications.

1. Each person is dealing with his own problems as his. They aren't the other's. It isn't the other's failure if we fail in an area we aren't strong in.

2. Both members love and appreciate the gifts of the other person. However, they see the other's gifts as gifts, not as necessities to the relationship.
3. Each member is actively involved in pursuing spiritual completion and growth in his areas of weakness, not content to let the other do the work in that area.

What Happens When Oppositeness Rules

Though opposites do attract, they can have their dangers as well. To illustrate the problems involved when opposites attract, we will use the example of Kim and Pete, a couple who dated for about a year. Their struggles will show what kinds of problems occur when oppositeness rules.

Kim always found it hard to relate to people. She had difficulty opening up to or trusting others. She began dating Pete, who had never met a stranger. People were always hanging around Pete, who seemed to naturally put people at ease with a smile or a question. Kim loved being with Pete, not only because she was attracted to him, but because good things happened when he was around. All of a sudden Kim found herself having lots of friends, due to her association with her opposite, Pete. They became a popular couple in their circles. Church events, parties, and sports events became a wonderful part of her life. Then, over the next few months, several things happened to the couple.

Loss of Freedom

First, Kim began realizing she had to schedule her life around Pete. When he wasn't around, she couldn't engage with others as freely because the chemistry wasn't there. So for Kim to have people in her life, she had to follow Pete around. She began losing freedom and control in her time and schedule.

When you depend on another person for what you should be developing, you no longer have control or freedom in that aspect of your life. It now belongs to the other person. Even if it is a good person who loves you, it is not you. God has designed you to make free choices in life (Galatians 5:1–2). When you are dependent on your date's oppositeness, you are no longer in charge. He has what you haven't developed, so you must give up freedom in order to get it from him.

Resentment

Kim and Pete found themselves resenting each other. Kim felt like a puppy without a life of her own, and felt that Pete controlled her. She also envied his ease of relating to others. Pete, on the other hand, began to resent Kim for her dependency on him. He didn't like having, as he put it, to "carry the social burden all the time." Though they cared for each other, these negative feelings began to get in the way of their relationship.

Confusion in Responsibilities

Kim began spending more and more of her life passively doing what Pete wanted. She began thinking her role in their relationship was to keep Pete happy, so he would keep her in social circles. The couple began a strange job-share that married couples find themselves in: Kim stopped taking responsibility for her friendships, and made Pete her project. Pete stopped taking responsibility for how he conducted his relationship with Kim. He knew she'd be around no matter what. Neither party was taking full ownership of their lives.

Parent-Child Struggles

Kim started feeling like she was the child and Pete the domineering parent. Since she desperately needed him around to maintain relationships, she would feel one-down to him when they differed in social engagement areas. If she wanted to go to a church singles social, and Pete wanted to go to a hockey game, they both knew she had more to lose than he did. Pete sometimes unfairly took advantage of his leverage, saying, "Well, you go to yours and I'll go to mine," knowing Kim would feel out of her element at the social without him. She felt he called the shots. Pete thought Kim was becoming pouty and immature, which is how parents often feel about a dependent child.

The other aspect of the parent-child struggle is that kids are designed by God to one day leave home. Their dependency on their "opposite" parents—that is, people who have strengths that the children don't yet possess—should one day resolve. At that point, they go out on their own.

This same reality happens in relationships, because the "opposite" issue is really about dependency. Ultimately it ended Kim and Pete's connection. Kim began to work on her shyness and trust problems. She got into a support group and began taking risks and opening up to others. She encountered lots of fears, but, in time, she began entering the world of relationships on her own. She actually found herself making friends of her own. No longer were Kim and Pete opposites. They were simply adults.

Kim began feeling freer to disagree with Pete about events and schedules, as she was no longer afraid to be without him. She began going to events with or without him. And, though he had resented Kim's dependency, Pete began resenting her independence more. Finally, the couple broke up. The parent-child stance they were in couldn't move into a grown-up, mutual one.

Dependency and Growth

All this is not to say that we should not be dependent on each other. God created us to be dependent on himself and others. He says that that is a good thing: "But pity the man who falls and has no one to help him up!" (Ecclesiastes 4:10). If you have ever failed or fallen apart, and had no one to help you get up, you know how empty that sort of life is. Dependency on the love and support of others is a good thing. But dependency has an ultimate purpose: growth. We are to take in the love, comfort, and instruction of others in order to grow spiritually and emotionally.

The problem is that you can have a relationship that has dependency, but no growth. The dependency is regressive. It keeps you or your date unformed emotionally. This is the problem of two opposites depending on the strengths of each other. Two people are close, supportive, and connected. But someone isn't doing the hard work of taking what they are given and working on their character and soul. *Dependency that does not lead to growth ultimately creates more immaturity in the person.* At some point, babies are weaned. Kids are told to jump in the pool. And young adults learn to make moral and career decisions for themselves.

Hugh and Sandy had been dating for a while. He was an organized business type. She was an artistic person, with interests in painting, acting, and music. He was fascinated by her creativity. Sandy brightened up his otherwise predictable, left-brained life. For her, Hugh brought a stability and safety that she needed. Though they initially appreciated each other's strengths, they inadvertently and quickly began to depend on each other for their own deficits. Hugh stopped trying to be a more emotional and spontaneous person, and left it to Sandy. In her stead, Sandy stopped trying to organize her life and let Hugh deal with it.

As the relationship progressed, however, cracks began to show. Hugh began to resent having to deal with Sandy's financial crises, chronic scheduling problems, and career issues. He felt he was having to parent her. From Sandy's view, she resented having to be interesting to a dull, somewhat controlling person, and felt she was doing all the emotional giving in the relationship. They were both right. They were using dependency to serve immaturity, not growth.

Opposites often depend on each other. That is not a problem, as long as that dependency spurs each member on to maturity and completeness.

Opposites and Maturity

In our experience, the degree of attraction that opposites have for each other is often diagnostic of the couple's maturity. In mature couples, opposite traits are simply not a major issue. The two people are not drawn to opposite traits due to their own deficits. They are drawn to values that they share, such as love, responsibility, forgiveness, honesty, and spirituality. Attraction based on values is much more mature than attraction based on what you don't have inside.

On the other hand, immature couples seem to struggle more with finding someone who possesses the nurturance, structure, competence, or personality that they don't. They go through painful cycles of idealizing the other person, getting closer, developing a dependency on the other person, making a parent out of them, then having horrible breakups, only to look for someone again with those opposite traits. Ultimately, many are looking for a parent to take care of part of them that they aren't taking care of in themselves.

Differences can help make a good relationship fulfilling, rich, and satisfying. Each partner appreciates the talent and unique points of view of the other, and falls more deeply in love with that person. The couple becomes part of the wonder of love, that two people who are so opposite can connect so well, and become truly one.

My father, who has been married for fifty years to my mother, is very different from her. He likes playing jazz piano in the background for her while she sings. He still talks about how she can light up a room with her presence, while he enjoys being in the background. What he is actually saying, I think, is that she lights up not only the room, but also his own heart. And that is how opposites truly can attract: not as a basis for a relationship, but as a wonderful complement and addition to an already loving connection.

So make oppositeness a nonissue. Look more for character, love, and values than "who has what." Don't fall for an introvert simply because you are an extrovert. Fall for someone who calls you into love, growth, and God. And then appreciate her unique differences.

Take-Away Tips

Let's end this section with a few suggestions to deal successfully with the "oppositeness rules" problem.

- Reserve your dating life for people actively involved in the growth process. Those who are taking ownership of their deficits are less likely to develop dependencies on the strengths of others.
- Be in the growth process yourself. Growth attracts growth. You will find yourself more drawn to others for healthy reasons, and less attracted to others because of what you don't possess.
- Make a distinction between attraction to a person based on your deficits, or someone's attraction to you based on his deficits, and attraction to a person's uniqueness and differentness.
- Make sure your dating relationship involves both love and truth. Challenge each other to grow. If your relationship is one of total comfort, you may be contributing to each other's spiritual laziness.
- Set boundaries on your tendencies to rescue each other from your character deficits. If you are the connector,

like Pete, don't do all the relational work for your date. If you are the assertive one, like Alex, don't enable your date by doing all the confronting. Encourage, but don't rescue.

- Normalize and identify each of your character deficits. Such issues as detachment, irresponsibility, overresponsibility, perfectionism, authority conflicts, and the like, should be topics that you both can talk about personally, about yourself and each other. Two good sources of information about these issues are *Changes That Heal* by Dr. Cloud and *Hiding from Love* by Dr. Townsend. Be agents of growth, healing, and change for each other, specifically in these issues.

Part Three

Solving Dating Problems: When You're Part of the Problem

Chapter 10

Adapt Now, Pay Later

To put it mildly, Keri was star-struck. She had a feeling when she met Steve that he was different. "Handsome, successful, spiritual, loves kids" could have been his personal ad. He was everything that she had been looking for, and she could not believe that "God had brought him" into her life. She was floating on clouds.

When they went on their first date, she liked how he took control. He had the evening completely planned out and seemed to take care of every detail. It gave her such a secure feeling just to be around someone who was so in charge. As the evening went on, she could tell that this was not just another someone, but the kind of person that she wanted to get to know better. That night when he dropped her off, she felt tingly inside.

It surprised her when he called the next morning. "I had a great time last night. Let's do it again this afternoon," he said. There was that "in charge" thing again, and she liked it just as much the next day as the first night. "Sure. What do you want to do?" she asked.

"I have some tickets to the game and we could do dinner afterwards. Pick you up at noon," Steve told her.

Hesitating a bit, Keri nevertheless said, "I'll be ready." She hung up the phone, surprised at how quickly she had said yes, for she knew that she had plans for dinner with some friends. But how could she refuse? She did not want to give him the wrong signal, that she was not interested. Besides, her friends would understand. After all, they would probably go out and talk about how difficult it had been lately to find quality guys, and she thought it would make a lot more sense to go out with one than to talk about it. So she called and let them know.

When Steve picked her up, they seemed to click all over again. They had a great afternoon and then were on their way to dinner when he asked, "How about Chinese food? I know a great place near here."

"Sounds great," Keri said. Inside, she cringed. She hated Chinese food with a passion, kidded her friends when they ate it, and had all sorts of derogatory names for it. But, after all, she did not want to argue about something so small. Nor did she want to ruin the evening when, after dinner, Steve suggested that they go for a walk around the lake. Dead tired, and with an early appointment the next morning, Keri agreed. She dared not say no.

Little did Keri know that this was a foreshadowing of what was to come. Over time, she began to notice that every time Steve suggested something, she complied. She was jelly in his hands. Falling in love day by day, she was interested only in being with him, and whatever he liked or wanted to do was fine as long as they were together.

But, after about two months, there was a gnawing in her stomach that was beginning to bother her. In the very beginning of the relationship (and some of this is normal), she had not cared about little things such as time constraints, other commitments, having different preferences, and things that might cause conflict. It mattered so much to her to not chase Steve away or be difficult for him, that she just would comply. But it was beginning to not work for her as she had other things to do and some of her own preferences that were not finding room in their decision-making.

It began with her work. A freelance writer, she was getting behind in her work as she spent more and more time with him. So, slowly, she began to say that she had to go write or go research a story. It was the same with her friends. Gradually, she was missing them and began to want to spend time with them. So she started to say no to some of Steve's requests. In addition, she was beginning to want to do other things than the ones that he would suggest.

At first, he was fine with her working. But, before long, he began to get upset with her when she would make choices that would take her away from him or that were different than he wanted. He would get irritated and short with her, and sometimes she felt like he was not very mature.

Finally things came to a head when she had to go on a trip to cover a story for a magazine and he did not want her to go. "This just does not work for me," he told her. "You have to make a choice. It is either going to be your work or me. I cannot come behind your work all the time." And then he drove off.

Keri was heartbroken and quick to blame herself. She saw her friend Sandy and told her what had happened, and was full of confessions. "He is right. I just can't expect to have my own career and keep someone happy at the same time. I will have to find another way to work. I just hope I have not lost him."

But as Sandy listened to the story, and had witnessed some of it over recent months, she was seeing a pattern. As long as Keri had been adaptive to Steve and his wishes and wants, things went smoothly. But as soon as she had begun to be a real person with needs and desires of her own, he was unable to deal with the equality. It was his way or the highway.

Sandy was honest with her friend, something that was risky. She knew how much Keri was attached to Steve, but she loved Keri and had to tell her the truth. Sandy told Keri that she had not been herself with Steve. In fact, Keri was no longer the person that Sandy knew and respected.

Sandy said, "You are wrong in thinking that you can't have your career and have a relationship too. After all, you have to work! Steve liked you, but only when you were doing what he liked. Has he ever adapted himself to what you'd like? I think that you need to stand your ground and find out what kind of person he really is."

The truth was hard for Keri to hear. But she stood her ground with her friend's support and Steve did not like it. When she told him that there were going to be times that she would have to work and that she might not be there as much as she had been in the beginning, he could not take it. He said that it proved that she did not really care about him and their relationship, and that they did not want the same things after all.

Keri was devastated at first, but through the help of friends like Sandy, she realized that she had avoided a train wreck. Better to find out in the early months of a relationship that you are with someone who cannot adapt to your wishes than to find out much later, or God forbid, after marriage. She was grateful, and she had learned a lesson: *don't be someone you are not just to gain someone's love.* If you do, the person that your loved one is loving is not you. It is the role that you are playing and not your true self who is being loved.

Wishes, Needs, and Desires

As Keri discovered, you cannot act forever. As one of my counselees said one day about his relationship with his wife, "At some point I always screw up and have an opinion." It just happens. *You are a person, and you cannot go throughout life without pur-*

suing your own wishes, needs, and desires, nor should you. Your needs and desires are going to come out, and you had better find out early in the relationship where the person you are dating really stands with the idea of sometimes having to adapt to them.

Otherwise, you will be in the situation that Keri found herself in. She adapted early and gave Steve a false idea of who she was. Then, as she began to be who she really was, there was a problem. He thought he was getting a really compliant woman who would do whatever he wanted, whenever he wanted. And she was adding to that illusion by her behavior. When the truth came out, there was trouble. Sometimes the truth takes years to come out, but it always happens and it is never pretty.

Take it from us. As marriage counselors, we see many, many marriages that get into trouble with this dynamic. One person has very poor boundaries when the relationship begins and the other has all the control. Then after some amount of time in the marriage, the compliant one cannot take it anymore. He or she finally stands up and wants to be a person. And many times the spouse, who is more often than not self-centered, does not like it. The rules are changing and the spouse does not have the tools to deal with the change. And the marriage gets into trouble. Sometimes it grows, sometimes it adapts, and sometimes it does not.

The key to remember is that the only reason that a marriage like that exists in the first place and has gone on like that is *that one person adapted from the beginning.* If that person had had boundaries, like Keri found, the marriage never would have happened. Or if it did, the problem would have been fixed first.

Make sure that you do not end up in a relationship that turns into a bad marriage. You don't want to be telling some counselor the following things ten years from now:

- She seems to have to have her way.
- I am afraid to let my real feelings and desires be known.

- We have so much conflict over such little things.
- We always spend our money on what he wants.
- She doesn't care about me and what I want.
- Why can't he ever go to the places that I want to go to?

Issues like these are usually discovered later in a relationship where one partner has adapted for a long time, and then makes a change. The lesson of this chapter is to *be yourself from the beginning*, and then you can find someone who is authentic as well. A relationship like that has mutuality and partnership. It has give and take. It has equality. It has sharing and mutual self-sacrifice for the sake of the other and the relationship. If you are a real person from the start, a relationship of mutuality has a chance of developing. If you are not, then you might be headed for trouble.

Bad Attractions

The question of many singles is "Why do I keep attracting such jerks?" They think that something is inherently wrong with them, and sometimes they can begin to get quite hopeless over their chances of finding someone good to date or marry.

People who are selfish and controlling can only be that way if they are in relationship with someone who is adaptive. If someone stands up to them and is honest about his or her wants and desires, then the controlling person has to learn to share or gets frustrated and goes away.

The little things in life are where you can spot the big things. If you are with a self-centered person who cannot give to your desires, you will find out soon enough by being honest and straightforward about simple things, for that is where day-to-day life is lived. You will quickly find out if you are with someone who is able to share, or someone who has to have his or her way all the time. This knowledge will be helpful now and essential for the future.

Take-Away Tips

- Tell the truth about where you want to go and not go, or what you want to do or not do.
- Be honest about your preferences and desires.
- Don't act like you like things that your date likes just so that you will be accepted. Being liked for who you are requires that you be that person.
- Don't be afraid to share your desires and wants for fear of conflict. Find out early if you are with someone who can share equally.
- Get feedback from honest friends to tell you if you are really being yourself and seeing the relationship realistically.
- Remember with each decision that you make you are giving the other person an impression of what you like in life and in a relationship. Be careful—he or she might believe you.
- When you give or serve, let it be honest and purposeful.

Chapter 11

Too Much, Too Fast

*O*ne of my (Dr. Townsend's) closest friends, Chuck, is a talented songwriter. When we were college buddies, I was visiting him in his room one day. Chuck picked up his guitar and said, "Want to hear my new love song?" I said I did, and he sang me the following: "I love you. Always have, always will. What's your name?"

I never found out whether Chuck was referring to his dating history or simply observing college romantic life, but I knew I could identify with his lyrics. I understood the ritual of intense professions of undying love, followed by the realization of utter ignorance about one's beloved. In other words, too much, too fast.

The problem of premature commitment and overinvolvement in a dating relationship is a common one. Two people find that they have strong feelings for each other. In a short period of time, they begin investing enormous amounts of time in the relationship. They suspend or neglect other people, interests, and activities. They quickly start dating exclusively. They feel intense passion for each other, and miss each other deeply when they are apart. They may marry soon thereafter, or they may break up, only to repeat the fast pace with someone else. Either way

the relationship resolves itself, the couple is typified by a driven-
ness to become highly committed, a process that takes less than
a normal amount of time.

What is normal? While the Bible is not explicit on the issue
of how long a dating relationship should go on, we would suggest
that a year, not including the engagement period, is a good min-
imum. We wouldn't consider two or three years unrealistic. We
know that God has set up a time and a season for every activity
under heaven (Ecclesiastes 3:1). When you date for at least a year,
you experience a good measure of the seasons of life that people go through: holidays, fiscal periods, vacations, school terms,
etc. You can observe how the relationship deals with the flow
of life of both people. This information is invaluable in helping
a couple see what kind of a "fit" they are.

Yet many people meet, date, and mate within a few months
or even weeks. They believe they have recognized the right person and think they are ready for marriage. Or some couples
will take the requisite year or two to date, but will have a problem in "frontloading" the relationship: they become deeply committed very soon in the game, and never go through a process
of gradually becoming closer over time. Either way, the issue
is the same. For a number of reasons that we will show, the
couple sees time as the adversary, and actively resists any more
of it than is necessary.

Why Wait?

Youth specialist Josh McDowell asked that question to millions of teens about saving sex for marriage. The same question applies to the issue of pacing how quickly to get involved
in your dating relationship: why should you wait, take time, and
become closer in a gradual manner, to a person to whom you
are enormously attracted? There are some helpful answers to
that question below.

Relationships Do Not Tolerate Shortcuts

First we have to understand the nature of relationships as God designed them. This applies not only to dating, but families and friendships. Relationships grow in a healthy manner only as they undergo experiences, and there is no shortcut to experiences. In other words, we only "know" each other to the extent that we have experience with each other. We can know facts about the person we are dating: their friends, job, hobbies, and so forth. But that doesn't mean we "know" them as a person. That kind of "knowing" cannot come from reading a file on someone. For example, when Adam "knew" Eve (Genesis 4:1, in King James language), he was knowing her in experience, in the deep intimacy that comes in healthy sexuality.

Experience requires time. It is simply impossible to get enough experiences under your belt without spending a lot of time dealing with the relationship. Here are some examples of necessary time-consuming dating activities on the road to becoming committed to someone:

- Having enough talks to safely open up with each other
- Entering each other's worlds of work, hobbies, worship, and service
- Meeting and spending time with each other's friends
- Understanding each other's strengths and weaknesses
- Going over basic values of what is important in life to each other
- Getting to know each other's families
- Spending time away from each other to think through the relationship, alone and with friends
- Learning your best style of disagreement and conflict management

It's hard to imagine doing all that in a few months, because it can't be done. Yet so many dreamy-eyed couples will say to their friends, "You don't understand. It's as if we've known each other all our lives. We were soul mates from the first meeting." And, while I know people who have met and married quickly, I think their success is due more to their own character than to going through the process the right way.

For example, my Aunt Jonnie and Uncle Walton have been married over fifty years. I have seen his framed proposal of marriage to her. He wrote it to her when they were both in kindergarten! I guess they both knew each other was "The One" pretty early on in life. But I don't think they would attribute their successful marriage to how early they committed. Knowing and observing them all my life, I think they would instead talk about love, the right values, their faith, and being able to go through good times and bad together.

There is no microwave dating that makes any sense. Go through the seasons of life with the person you believe might be the one God has meant for you.

A *Measure of Importance*

Secondly, the time involved in dating someone should reflect the significance of the relationship. Simply put, the more important a decision is, the more time it should take to make it. This sounds obvious, but many couples miss the mark here. We spend many years deciding on a career. We wrestle for long periods over committing to our faith. We research financial dealings for months. It makes sense that our most important human relationship should also warrant the time due it.

So many married couples look back on their dating lives and regret that they did not take more time to evaluate, question, explore, and challenge issues with each other. When you are dating, it is hard sometimes to think beyond the warm, deep, and romantic feelings the relationship may elicit. But few decisions in life are more profoundly life-changing than marriage. Look at some of the significant aspects of marriage:

- A lifelong commitment to loving one person only
- Forsaking all other opportunities for romantic love other than that person
- Being in relationship with all the bad, immature, and broken parts of that person
- Having your own bad, immature, and broken parts open to the scrutiny of that person
- Solving conflict in ways that do not involve leaving the relationship
- Staying in the relationship even if the other person changes for the worse
- Being called to sacrifice many individual preferences for the sake of the relationship

This list isn't meant to depress you, but to help you see the gravity of what dating is meant to produce. To make a hasty, impassioned, or reactive decision can be disastrous. All things being equal, a bad marriage is probably more painful than a bad single state. Why? Because in a bad marriage, the structure of intimacy is in place, but it does not have the heart of intimacy. Two people live their lives together—intertwined by being in the same house, sleeping in the same bed, and raising the same children—yet emotionally they live alone. Living alone within the marriage contract makes the disconnection feelings so acute that many people leave the marriage. With such serious factors at stake, it is worth it to take ample time to get to know someone.

The Nature of Love

Another reason to take your time is that this is a necessary part of learning how to love. Dating should not only produce a mate, it should also develop within you the ability to love that mate deeply and well. Love as the Bible defines it is a stance of working for the best for another person. God's love moved him to send his Son for our best (John 3:16). When we learn how to date the right way, that sort of love is born and grows within us.

For example, when you pace your relationship, you are giving up things you would like now for a greater benefit later. You are tolerating delay of gratification, experiencing frustration, and learning patience. You are learning to care for a person who does not belong to you yet, which is an anxiety-provoking situation.

Basically, taking time in your dating relationship helps you clarify the distinction between need and love. Both are about seeking relationship, and both are good aspects of life, but they are often confused. Need seeks closeness to fill up our deficits, such as loneliness, dependency, or powerlessness. Love seeks closeness for its own sake, knowing that the other person benefits from the relationship.

If you are dating someone who is pressing you to commit earlier than you would like, ask him why he wants to. Unless you are a total commitment-phobic person, most of his reasons will probably involve some need he has, such as:

- Needing the security of knowing he has your total commitment
- Wanting to end the sexual frustration
- Needing the relationship in order to feel complete
- Needing someone to relate to in his life

These desires may involve good needs, but they are no reason for speeding up things. They all involve some sort of dependency, and put you in a parental role at some level. As we will see many times in this book, one of the worst things you can do is try to reparent someone you are dating. It usually causes confusion and pain for both parties.

Remember to use gradual, well-paced dating to not only seek love, but also to become loving: "Love is patient" (1 Corinthians 13:4).

Am I Going Too Fast?

It can be difficult to tell if you are going too fast. Love does have an individual pace for people. Some can safely progress more quickly than others. They may be better decision-makers, or be more mature in relationships than others. Also there is such a thing as going too slow. Consider the plight of the woman who has dated a commitment-phobic guy for years with no hope of progress.

Here are some ways of determining if you are committing too quickly:

- You "know" each other emotionally more than you "know" each other objectively.
- You find yourself more invested in the relationship than in areas of your life that are important to you.
- You abruptly stop dating others.
- You get feedback from friends that this seems to be going quickly.

Whatever the signs, pay attention to them. As a rule of thumb, it is better to err on the side of caution.

Why We Don't Wait

If there are such benefits to dating at a gradual pace, then why do we see so much overinvolvement? There are lots of reasons people dive into the shallow end of love. Here are some of the main ones.

Loneliness

Loneliness is one of the most painful yet necessary experiences in life. People feel incomplete, empty, or even starving inside. It is also a strong motivating force, just as food hunger is. Loneliness can make us do almost anything to fill up the hole inside. It is easy to see how, when you find someone you are drawn to, you can quickly fill your life up with that person.

Loneliness is stronger than resolve, willpower, or discipline. People will promise themselves not to get too involved, and find that their promise melts when their relational hunger meets a person they desire. All of a sudden, they are spending every evening together and settling into a pattern of being a couple.

Loneliness is not the enemy here, however. When we are lonely, it is a signal that we are alive. God created us with the drive to connect and be attached to himself and others. It is a good thing, because loneliness ultimately leads us to relationship, and that is where God wants all of us. We are all members of one body (Ephesians 4:25). Relationship cures loneliness.

However, dating is not the kind of relationship that cures loneliness, and that is the real problem here. Relationships that resolve loneliness must have certain elements, such as safety, unconditional love, and deep commitment. These elements help the person take in the love they need, get connected to life, and stay in relationship. Dating does not have those elements. At least at first, it is exploratory and low-commitment in nature. So lonely people often get deeply and quickly connected to someone. Then, when conflicts arise, they are devastated because they invested such deep parts of their hearts and souls in the relationship.

If you are getting too close, too soon out of loneliness, use it as a signal to get connected with some good, solid, nondating relationships. Deal with loneliness before it backfires on you.

Difficulty in Leaving Home

Some couples will appear almost married at early stages of the courtship. They will rapidly establish themselves as a unit, with their own patterns and predictable schedule. They may seem settled and secure with each other. In some ways, it might look like a picture of what most people dream about—the lifetime soul mate.

However, there may be a darker nature to the picture. Sometimes a couple seems to "couple" very quickly because they have not finished the task of emotionally leaving home. They are unable to navigate single life and find that it is not working well for them. Thus, they are opting more for the marriage state than they are for the person.

One of the descriptions of an adult is a person who has effectively left home. It has to do with moving out of dependency on one's family, and becoming autonomous and responsible for oneself. Everyone needs a transition period in early adulthood in which they gradually take what they have gleaned from home and create a life for themselves away from home. This is why the college and early twenties years are so important: they provide a context to learn how to live life on one's own.

Leaving home applies not only to the "doing" areas of life, such as finances, career decisions, and homebuilding, but also the "relating" areas of life. Adults move out of emotional dependency on their family. They love them, but they no longer need them as they used to. This prepares them for the "leaving and cleaving" process (Genesis 2:24) that God has designed for us. We move away from the family of origin and create our own family—in friendships, work, church, and neighborhoods.

Singleness is a struggle for those who have not finished leaving home. They do not enjoy it, and may feel it is an empty, cold, or unsafe way to live. They are still, at some level, yearning for the home environment that they never finished leaving. And that is why they often commit so quickly. Marriage is the only way they can experience being "home." This becomes a problem when, after they have married, the dependencies surface in other ways. For example, one person becomes totally dependent on another. Or one still prefers Mom and Dad over her spouse. Or one is now wanting more freedom from his spouse, as he is now ready to leave home.

This struggle applies not only to never-marrieds, but also to divorced folks. Many divorced people will overcommit because they are more used to the married state. As one previously married woman told me, "I married my ex-husband when I was nineteen, and we were married thirty years. I don't know the rules of singleness." In this problem, it is often good to separate out the person from the lifestyle.

Difficulties in Sustaining Friendships

Some people will overcommit due to problems in making deep, sustaining friendships. They will find that they don't feel a part of life and can't get truly close to people. It may be hard for them to trust others. They struggle with what are called attachment issues. People with attachment issues may not feel lonely. In fact, they may feel relief when they are alone, as their need for relationship has been cut off.

I have a friend who is one of the most talented drawing artists I have ever met. He draws breathtaking scenes. Yet he couldn't talk to anyone about anything but art. Intimacy was an area he had little experience in. Then, at nineteen, he met a girl who was highly relational and outgoing. He fell quickly in love with her, and they became inseparable, marrying in a few months. I asked him what attracted him to her, and he said, "She makes it easy to talk and relate. It's hard with others." I can appreciate that, but I have also seen, over the years, her resentment at being the only conduit to life that her husband has.

Perfectionism

You would think that perfectionists would never marry, being too picky. They would be fearful of making a mistake, or forever worried they'd committed to someone who was okay, then encounter the perfect person around the corner. Yes, sometimes a perfectionist will delay commitment. But being driven by ideals can also cause the opposite problem of committing too quickly. This is because people deal with their perfectionism in different ways.

For example, some perfectionists become quickly committed to a person who seems to represent every weakness they don't have. Their friends will scratch their heads in bewilderment, and try to adapt to someone that none of them have anything in common with. This is often because the perfectionist, being unable to resolve her own weaknesses, badness, and imperfections, will instead quickly fall in love with someone who possesses them. She projects what she is unable to tolerate in herself onto her beloved. In this way, she is still in relationship with all of the parts of herself, yet she doesn't have to take ownership of them.

When you see the "angel" woman quickly committing to "devilish" guys, this is one of the likely causes. What is not worked on in our souls is often found in those we choose.

What Should I Do?

If your dating life tends to be too much, too fast, there are several things you can do about it. They are not enjoyable, and involve some work. But if you are tired of the roller coaster of intense but failed relationships, it is worth it.

Identify What Is Driving the Pace

It could be loneliness, fear of being out in the world, problems in making friends, or perfectionism. Work on these issues as life issues, not as dating problems. As you mature in these areas, the frenzy will often resolve itself.

Get a Life

A full life is probably the best antidote for getting too close, too fast. Nature abhors a vacuum, and people tend to fill up emptiness with romantic commitment. Ask God to help you get involved in real life: spending time on friends, work, hobbies, church, service, and God himself.

Deliberately Slow the Pace to Diagnose the Relationship

If you can slow your pace, you will quickly find out what is underneath the speedy commitment. For example, the other person may become frustrated and impatient, as he doesn't want to deal with the problems between you. Or you may find anxious, sad, or angry feelings welling up that the fast pace has protected you from. If the relationship is mature, it will withstand the test of slowing down.

Investigate Who Is Contributing to the Pace

Does it tend to be you, those you date, or both? This helps you find out where the pressure is coming from, and do something about it.

Ask Friends for Feedback

Humbly go to mature, safe friends and ask them to tell you when you're getting weird. When they see that crazed look in your eye, and you are preparing to heavily invest in someone quickly, give them permission to say, "Stop!"

It is easy to get overcommitted quickly in the world of dating. However, resolving what is driving that pace can provide a more balanced and healthy dating life.

Take-Away Tips

- If the relationship is moving quickly, look at that as a signal and ask yourself why.

- Avoid the tendency toward too-quick involvement by getting involved with each other's real lives, especially friendships.
- Deal with conflicts, differences, and preferences instead of glossing them over.
- Remember that quick, intense relationships often end up either burning out or being shallow. Real love takes time and has no shortcut, but it is worth it.
- Make sure you're not moving quickly because you are avoiding some other pain, such as loneliness or inner hurt.
- Ask God to make you patient with the process of love, and to be able to experience its growth day by day.

Chapter 12

Don't Get Kidnapped

*D*ebbie was getting to a pretty good place in her growth. She had been working on some issues in her life and had been very successful with the support system that she had developed. Having struggled with a few difficult relationships and some self-image problems, she was happy to be getting to a new place in her life.

She had not dated anyone seriously since she and her fiancé had had a tough breakup a year before. It was at that time that she turned to her friends for healing and stability. And it had paid off. Debbie was having a good time with her friends and feeling good about life and the future. She had gotten active in her spiritual life and church, as well as pursuing some new hobbies and interests. She had learned to sail and was taking some art classes. Most of her social life was spent dating different people and hanging out with her friends. And she was really beginning to find fulfillment in some community projects that she had volunteered for. Life was getting good again.

Then she met Nick. They hit it off right away and began spending a lot of time together. Soon they were dating exclusively. At first her friends were excited for her that she had found someone that she liked so much. They kidded her about being "lost at sea," and other metaphors for not seeing her very much. It seemed that Nick was becoming her whole life. But for her, her new relationship with Nick seemed like the next step in her life becoming everything she had wanted.

But as time went on, her friends weren't laughing anymore. They were sad because they rarely saw Debbie. They would occasionally talk to her on the phone, but it seemed that she was always on her way out to do something with Nick, or was at his house, or something like that. They were excited for her, but they missed her as well. Finally, they just settled in to the fact that she was in love and they had seen the last of her for a while. They were also unhappy because they were really not getting to know him either. On a few occasions, they had met him, but they never really did things with Nick and Debbie. The group activities that all of them had done for so long were not happening anymore, so Nick was somewhat of a mystery to Debbie's circle of friends.

Meanwhile, from Debbie's perspective, everything was wonderful. They loved doing things together and were enjoying getting to know each other better. Debbie knew that she was falling in love.

What she did not see was that she was gradually changing, or being changed. Once strongly interested in so many outside activities and hobbies, she mostly just hung out with Nick and did whatever he wanted to do. He was an avid surfer, and she would spend a lot of her time at the beach, watching and reading. The community work that she had spent a lot of time investing in was not getting any of her attention anymore, nor was her group who had been such a big part of her growth. But she was so "happy," that she did not really miss any of it.

Spiritually, it seemed that all her interest in God had gone away. It wasn't that she had turned her back on him; she was simply consumed with Nick. She found herself thinking little about God or spiritual growth anymore. But she was so "happy."

Things continued like this until two things happened that served as a wake-up call for Debbie. First, she began sleeping with Nick, something that she had vowed not to do again until she was safely married. Her vow was part of her spiritual commitment to God and also wisdom she had learned from her previous breakup. What had looked like it would be "forever" had not been after all, and she felt devastated that she had given herself away to someone who had ultimately used her. Now, she found herself doing the same thing again, although this time, she had assured herself, was really going to be forever. But as time went on, her duplicity was beginning to gnaw at her. And she also didn't like how casually Nick was taking their sex life. In the beginning, he had seemed so spiritually committed. But, as she was finding out, his spirituality did not have very deep roots.

The second wake-up call was one day when Nick asked her if she would be interested in looking into cosmetic surgery. At first she thought he was kidding. But when she laughed it off, he did not and pursued it further. "I just think it would help your overall looks," he said.

Debbie was devastated, but more than that, she began thinking. She began to remember other conversations that she and Nick had had about her. Some were about her looks, her hair, at times her weight. (She was a very normal and attractive weight.) Others were about her wardrobe and style, and as she thought more about it, others were about significant areas of her life. She remembered his criticism of sailing when she first shared her excitement about her new passion. He thought it was boring and not where the real action was. That is how he ended up surfing a lot with her watching. Surfing was not boring, according to Nick.

But as she really began to think about it, watching surfing was not that exciting either. She had just been so happy to be near Nick that she had lost touch with her interests.

There were other subtle criticisms as well about her other interests. He was not mean at all about them, which is probably why she did not notice that it was happening. It was more of a combination of thinking that things she liked or wanted were not really that great, or more often, he just had a better way of doing things or better things to do.

The same thing had been true about her friends. He had not really clicked with them that much, and that was part of why she had gotten so separated from them. He would say things about her friends like, "she's a little too artsy for me," or other comments that were not really put-downs, but enough to show that he was not interested in the people that she loved. But, again, *she had missed it because being with him was what mattered to her.* She just felt so good to be with him that pushing him into things or people that he did not like was not a priority to her. She loved being with him. And, this was the subtlety, he was great to be around.

He was fun, positive, pleasant, and so much more. So, it was not as if he had been mean and critical. He just had subtly negated most of the people and things that were important to her. She was beginning to see that now. Nick was a strong personality, which was part of what she loved about him. But that strength was not directed in pursuing her life and desires as much as his own. As a result, she saw that she had lost touch with her values as well as a lot of the things that she loved. It was surprising to her how much she had given in to his loving control.

The rest of Debbie's story was not easy, but fortunately had a good ending. Thanks to the cosmetic surgery comment, she went to talk to a few of her friends. She opened up about the physical comments and cosmetic surgery suggestion, as well as the way that she had lost touch with a lot of her hobbies and

other things that were important to her. She told them that she
was sleeping with Nick as well. The friends had all covenanted
with each other to be available for support to one another in that
area if it were needed. Debbie was sad that she had not taken
advantage of her friends' support earlier.

But, now it was there, and she was seeing the need for their
help in seeing reality. At that point, they did what friends are
supposed to do. They were very direct. And enraged. It is interesting sometimes to see how the people who love someone often
express the anger that the person is unable to express themselves.

"What? Overweight? Is this guy crazy? Give me the phone.
I'll tell him what overweight is!"

"Cosmetic surgery? This guy is a loon. How could you just
sit there and take that?"

"What do you mean sailing is boring? You love sailing. Did-
n't you tell him to go walk off a pier and then see if he would like
to see you come sailing by?"

"He pushed you for sex after you told him how important it
was for you to wait? This guy is really selfish."

They were mad. And at first, Debbie was somewhat defensive
of Nick, telling them how nice he was and how he would never
be mean or mistreat her. But they were relentless and would not
allow her denial to continue. He was nice, but he was kidnap-
ping her. She was being separated from her friends, support systems, and everything that was important to her, even her values.

Slowly she began to get it. And she did what she should have
done earlier. She used her support network to ground her, and
from that position of strength she began to get stronger and more
direct with Nick. She returned to her strong stand on the limits of
their physical relationship, and she said that it was important that
he do some things with her friends, as well as go sailing with her.

Nick was not defensive. He said that he did not realize that
he was hurting her feelings by his comments and actions. He

said he was sorry. They decided to go forward from there. It looked good for a little while, but reality began to set in again as to his real nature and intentions, conscious or not. He was still bothered by her appearance, wanting her to change. He resentfully went to things she suggested, but it was not a joyful participation. There was new conflict.

But this time there was a huge element that made all the difference in the world: *Debbie stayed connected to her friends and community.* She spent time with them as well as Nick, and she went back to church and her activities. In her interactions with her friends, she could describe what was happening, and they were able to give her feedback. They were able to help her see the reality of this relationship, and finally she and Nick broke up.

Sound like a good ending? You bet it is. Debbie was spared much heartache that would have been certain if she had gone forward. Without the support of her friends, her need for a relationship just might have driven her to continue, even into marriage with Nick. Friends gave her several important ingredients that every dating relationship must have in order to be based in reality. Let's look at those ingredients here.

A Feedback Base to See Reality

Being "in love," in the beginning of a relationship, is an illness. It is treatable, but it is an illness nevertheless. The illness is the inability to see reality. For the very state of "being in love" is a state of idealization, where the other person is not really viewed through the eyes of reality. He or she is mostly seen through the eyes of someone's own wishes or fantasies that the other person is able to symbolize. But often the fantasies are based on enough reality that the stage of idealization can move to something real and lasting.

The problem is that if the idealizations are strong enough, and the person's need for them to be true are strong enough, then he or she can omit large chunks of reality about the person he is in love with. This is why staying connected to a group of friends who know you well is so important. Your friends and often family can see things about your new love that you will not be able to see. And you should trust them. Unless there is something wrong in your relationships with them, or they are particularly dysfunctional, they will not be looking through the eyes of idealization and need and will see the person more clearly. Have you ever wondered how some people that you know and love were able to pick the difficult, or sometimes awful person that they are with? Do you think that the prince just one day turned into a frog? Most times not. The frog was always a frog, even if he was dressed up like a prince in courtship. But the princess was looking through the eyes of idealization or denial. Borrow your friends' vision. You might need it.

Also, they know you, and they know what is important to you. They can see if you are becoming a more well-rounded, complete *you* with this person, or if you are becoming someone other than yourself. They know who you are and will be able to see if you are growing into more of who God created you to be.

These two things were drastically missing in Debbie's relationship with Nick. Because they did not do things with her friends and family, and because she was not staying close to her friends, she could not see the two realities that were occurring: her idealization of a controlling person, and her becoming someone other than who she really was. Her friends could have told her that along the way if she had stayed connected to them.

A Support Base to Deal with Reality

We do not deal with reality for two reasons. Either we do not see it, or we see it and are unable or unwilling to deal with it. Many times we will know that there is something wrong in a relationship and that we need better or different boundaries.

Sometimes we even know that the relationship is stupid or sinful. But we cannot find it in ourselves to break away or do the right thing.

That is where the power of a support system is needed. As Ecclesiastes 4:9–12 says, "Two are better than one, because they have a good return for their work: If one falls down, his friend can help him up. But pity the man who falls and has no one to help him up! Also, if two lie down together, they will keep warm. But how can one keep warm alone? Though one may be overpowered, two can defend themselves. A cord of three strands is not quickly broken." In part, we find the strength to do what we cannot do from the people who support us. They stand by us in difficult times to do several things:

- Give us emotional support.
- Give us truth and wisdom.
- Give us courage to take strong stands on values or morals.
- Give us courage to take strong stands with hurtful people.
- Give us comfort and strength to let go and grieve difficult situations or people.
- Give us knowledge and skills that we do not possess.

In Debbie's situation, she would have never been able to take the stand that she needed to take with Nick if her friends had not been there to support her. She was afraid of the conflict in the beginning and they gave her the strength to stand up and face it. Then, when it got worse, without them she probably would have caved in to Nick because she loved him, or needed him, so much. And finally, when she saw that this was a relationship that she did not want to go further in and she needed to break up, her friends helped her through the grief.

So many times, because of loneliness and abandonment feelings, a person will go through a breakup that is needed, and then go right back into the relationship to do it all over again. Friends and support systems provide the support you need to go through with a breakup. As Solomon says in Ecclesiastes 3:6, there is "a time to search and a time to give up; a time to keep and a time to throw away." Some dating relationships need to end and the time has come, but the person is not strong enough to do what is needed. Friends and community can be a lifesaver in that situation.

Connection to All the Parts of Her

As Debbie was dating Nick, she was losing parts of herself. That is not what happens in a good relationship. A good relationship helps us to become more of who God made us to be, not less. Slowly, Debbie was losing touch with not only her friends, but herself as well. She lost touch with her love of service and volunteer work. She lost touch with her passion for sailing and for art. She lost touch with her feelings for and drive to be close to God.

In addition, she was losing other aspects of herself. She generally was becoming a less well-rounded person and more one-dimensional. Her deeper spirituality had almost dried up completely as well as her full range of emotional responsiveness. Because she was losing touch with her life, she lost her ability to feel a lot of life's passions and emotions—her anger and her sense of protest had given way to dullness. Nick was all there was, and as a result there was a lot less of Debbie.

Her friends noticed this. They took her out to movies and museums. They listened to music and went to art shows with her. She took them sailing and she returned to her singles group at church, where she enjoyed many people and activities. Slowly, she was becoming herself again.

If she had been involved with her friends all along, she would not have lost these parts of herself, and would have found out earlier the problems with Nick. She would have stayed connected to all of who she was, and he would have had to be able to relate to her or at least not keep her from doing the things that she loved. If you are continuing to "do life" as you were before you started dating, you remain yourself, and the two of you get to know all of who each other is. Friends help you do that. They help you stay connected to the things you were connected with before you started dating.

The other side of this is that friends notice personality changes, for the better or the worse. How many times have you heard someone say, "Oh, she has grown so much since she stared dating _____. He just brings out the best in her." It is a beautiful thing and your friends will be able to see that. And how many times have you heard, "She has changed so much since she started dating _____. She is not herself. I don't even like to be around her anymore." Sometimes a dating relationship can change someone for the worse, too. Relationships have that kind of power when someone does not have good boundaries. It is up to friends to help give you that feedback if it is happening. It may be difficult to hear, but remember, "Wounds from a friend can be trusted" (Proverbs 27:6a). Sometimes we need to hear what our friends have to say about things that we cannot see.

Grounding in Spiritual Values That Make Life Work

Our spiritual values and our relationship with God ground us and make life work. He designed things that way. Our values are the architecture of life. They shape the way our life is going to be. If we value things like honesty, purity, compassion, sobriety, kindness, responsibility, and on and on, life will take on a certain shape that has a good end. However, when we begin to let our values slip, our life takes a different direction that does not have a good end. When Debbie began sleeping with Nick, she had lost a value that was very important to her and which also protected her from losing other aspects of herself. The pseudo-intimacy that they were having in sex was blinding her from seeing the lack of real intimacy in the relationship. That is one way that purity protects single people.

When she began to adapt to his perfectionistic physical demands on her looks and appearance, she lost touch with her honesty and value for kindness. What he was doing was not kind, and she should have honestly told him that she valued kindness in a relationship. His criticizing her physical appearance when she was perfectly normal was not a loving thing to do. We do not think that people should lie to each other. If she had a real problem, there would be nothing wrong with his telling her, or their talking about how it made him feel. But this was pure perfectionistic narcissism on his part. She should have kept her value of honesty and told him so.

Our community is one of the delivery systems that God has designed to help us stay grounded in our values and in him. We grow spiritually in those relationships, and God gives to us in those relationships as well (see Ephesians 4:16 and 1 Peter 4:10). Debbie's friends could have seen how she was losing her spiritual values and connection with God. They could have helped along the way. Fortunately for her, they did in the end. They confronted the ways that she was getting off the path of what was good for her. They did not do it in a condemning way, either. They did it like God does, with her best interests in mind.

Separateness and Development Apart from the Relationship

Every relationship involves two separate people with time and interests apart from each other. People who have no time, friends, or things they are into apart from the person they are dating probably are not being much of a whole person. You need your independence from each other. God made you that way. Debbie should have had time, space, friends, and interests alone, apart from Nick. And vice versa. But she got rid of her space and individuality and fused with him. Her friends would have been part of this separateness that would provide space and freedom from Nick, even if it had been going well.

A relationship that gets rid of one's individual life and friends, time and space, altogether is not a healthy relationship. It is more likely symbiotic and neurotic. Your friends are an important space-giving freedom that will help you to be healthier and more well-rounded. In addition, they will notice if you are losing them to a dating relationship. Debbie's friends came back into the picture and did that for her.

This is where dating other people can be very helpful. Especially in the early stages of a relationship, it is usually important to stay open to other people. That keeps you from getting caught up in some idealized fusion with someone and can keep you objective. You will notice that other people are different, for good or bad. And that comparison is helpful. It also reinforces to you that there are other fish in the sea and you won't feel like you "have to" land this particular one or you will be hopelessly alone. Keep your phone line open until you are sure who you are dealing with and that you really want to cut yourself off from other dating relationships.

Safe Dating

Remember, one aspect of safe dating is to remain connected to your friends and support system. A wolf attacks the lone sheep that has gotten away from the pack. Make sure that you are not vulnerable to what you cannot see, but with the help of other people, would otherwise be able to see very clearly. Stay connected, stay safe, and stay wise.

Some get kidnapped by controlling or dependent people. But others get kidnapped by their own wishes just to be close to someone. They give up all the things that are important because of their own lack of boundaries. Still others do not have enough of a community to get kidnapped away from. They are in a vacuum. Don't let any of these happen to you.

Work out your dating relationship with the help of the "support sandwich." See your friends as the bread, and your date as the filling. Spend time and energy with your dating relationships, but then return to your community. This especially becomes important if you have some strong stance to take or in time of conflict or change. Call a friend who knows the situation to give you courage before you go into it, go do the confrontation as planned, and then call them back for accountability. The sandwich may protect you in the areas where you do not have boundaries.

Take-Away Tips

- Don't even attempt to get serious in a dating relationship until you are connected to a good support system and friends who know you. If you are dating from a vacuum, you are in great danger.
- Stay involved with your friends and community as an individual, just like you were before you were dating this new person. You are still friends.
- Include the person you are dating in your circle of friends. If you are not, ask yourself why not? What it is about that person that does not fit in with your normal circle of friends? Make sure that you do a lot of things together with the group and other couples as well as alone.
- Be open and honest with your friends about what is going on in the relationship.

- Be spiritually accountable to your friends and stay involved in the spiritual community that is responsible for your growth.
- Be open to their feedback, even if it is difficult to hear. But weigh it and test it out with others who know you well. Do not depend totally on any one person's advice or feedback.
- Use your friends to lean on for support.
- Stay involved with your individual activities and time apart. Even if you begin to share the things you love, which is good, make sure you have some alone time and outside interests.
- Keep dating others until you are sure you want to commit to this one person. Don't get swept out of the pack too early.
- Use the "support sandwich."

Chapter 13

Kiss False Hope Good-bye

Control and judgmentalism were the two things that Robbie had been complaining about in his girlfriend for five solid years to all of his friends. He would be sure that she was the "one," but he could not commit to Melinda because of how she was in these two areas. And he was right. She was very controlling and she was very judgmental. He found himself either giving in to all of her wishes to avoid severe conflicts, and also hiding things about himself to avoid judgment. His friends had grown to the point where they could not stand her and hated what he was allowing her to do to him. Finally, they sent him to counseling, as they were getting tired of listening to him. So he came to see me (Dr. Cloud).

"But I love her," Robbie said. "She has so much about her that is so awesome. I cannot stand the thought of saying good-bye to her. She is so loving and smart and beautiful. In so many ways she is everything I want."

"Well, then stop complaining about her controlling nature and her judgmentalism, marry her, and be happy," I said. "But good luck."

"I can't do that. She will drive me crazy," he came back.

"Then you have a problem," I said.

"I know I do. I have to find a way to help her be more accepting and less judgmental, or be more patient until she finds it. Or, be more accepting, or something. But I don't think I can be happy marrying her with those things," he said. "And she is asking for a commitment."

"I don't think those things are what make up your problem. Your problem is that you have two incompatible wishes. You wish to be with someone who is not controlling, nor judgmental, *and* you wish to be with Melinda. Those two wishes are incompatible. As long as you have both of those, you are going to be miserable, as I see it. And the way you rationalize your misery is by thinking she is going to change. I believe in change," I told him. "Helping people change is my profession. But you have been dating her for five years, and as you describe the situation there is nothing in the picture that remotely points to her heading for change. So, change is out. Forget change. Pick one or the other of the wishes I described and get on with it."

Robbie just looked at me with a sad face. He did not like what I had told him and did not know what to do.

Hope is one of the greatest of virtues. As Paul says, "Faith, hope and love remain" (1 Corinthians 13:13). Hope drives great things to happen when all seems lost. If someone can keep hope going, then through faith and love, great things can be accomplished. Hope is surely a wonderful virtue, for without it, we give up and give in to all sorts of evil. We need it to persevere.

But the kind of hope that God wants us to have is the kind that "does not disappoint" (Romans 5:5), the kind that is based on the love that God has for us. God's love for us has been proven through his actions. We can go back to a point in history and say, "Look. It is true that God loves us. Here is a cross and an empty tomb. Hope in him makes sense. It is not false hope."

But the Bible speaks of another kind of hope as well. It is the hope that "makes the heart sick" (Proverbs 13:12). It is "hope deferred." In other words, hope that never is realized does not give life. It makes us sick and hopeless. It is a very good description of depression and giving up. When we hope and hope, and yet nothing happens and there is no reason to keep hoping other than hope itself, then despair settles in.

This is the kind of hope that Robbie had engaged in for five years. He had hoped that Melinda would change, but his hope was not a virtue at all. His hope was not based in any reality. It was denial and wishful thinking. And it was eating up his life. My job, as I saw it, was to get Robbie to give up hope and to either love Melinda as she was or move on. For I saw nothing in the picture that said that she was headed for change. There was no basis for his hope.

Good Hope and Bad Hope in Your Dating Life

What is the role of hope in dating? Some of you are probably saying, "I know—it is to hope for a date!" That might be true of some of you. But most of you who pick up this book probably are dating. And you are looking at the question of when to have hope that the person you are with is going to change. How should hope operate in that scenario?

To review, hope should be based in reality. Hope that will not disappoint has to be grounded in something more than wishing. It has to be grounded in more than just wanting a person or a situation to be different. There have to be some reasons to believe that things are going to change. Remember two truths:

1. The definition of crazy is to continue to do the same thing expecting different results.
2. The best predictor of the future, without some intervening variable, is the past.

If you examined your present situation, is your hope reasonable? Let's look at Robbie. He had, for five years, loved Melinda.

He had given to her. He had adapted to her. He had stopped adapting and confronted her. He had broken up with her. He had gone back with her. He had gone to counseling with her. He had tried everything. And yet he still had hope. Or was it a wish?

If he continued to do the above things, he would fit the definition for crazy, doing the same thing and expecting different results. That's truth number one. And truth number two says that Melinda won't change, because the best predictor of Robbie's next five years is the last five, without some intervening growth variable.

Chances are that some of you are struggling with whether or not you should give up hope on a certain relationship or continue in it. Let's take these two truths and apply them to some common scenarios.

The person you love treats you in a way that you cannot live with.

What do you do when the person you love treats you badly, or treats you in a way you can't live with? The normal path for changing something in a relationship is the following:

- Confront the dynamic. Tell the person what the behavior is, and how you feel when she does it.
- She listens, is not defensive, and owns the behavior.
- She empathizes with how it makes you feel and expresses sorrow.
- She apologizes and commits to not doing that anymore.
- With that repentance, there is true change and you do not see the behavior again. Or if she fails, she self-corrects, apologizes, is sorry, and continues on the path of repentance.
- She may occasionally fail, but overall there is a definite pattern of change and growth.

If there is not change after it is promised, then there is:

- Ownership by the person of the failure to change.
- Ownership of the inability to change on her own. She sees that her self-correction efforts are not working.
- She commits to doing more in order to change. That could be seeing a counselor, finding an accountability partner, joining a group, going to support meetings, or whatever. But there is more than just "trying harder" and relying on commitment and willpower. There is a looking for health. This may involve you as well, if the problem is a relationship problem.
- If it involves your changing as well, you are involved in the same process and working on your issues. You cannot blame another person if you are not treating her righteously. We must get the log out of our own eye first (Matthew 7:3–5).
- There is a gaining of insight into the patterns of what causes the problems and there is a difference in the path. There is not just a promise to not do it anymore, but an understanding of the causes and what sustains and drives the pattern.
- When there is a failure, there is more ownership and more insight. She returns to the system of help that she has sought out and uses it to confront the failure.
- There is less guilt and more sorrow. There is less self-attack and more problem solving.
- There is a sustained path of growth where you are not the driving force of motivation. In other words, the person is seeking change out of wanting to grow personally and out of care for the relationship. You are not having to "push" her any longer.

- Change begins to happen and is sustained. The failures are more and more infrequent and the responses are different. There is more sorrow and ownership, a return to the system, and an implementation of insight.
- If you are part of the dynamic, then you are following the same pattern.

If your loved one does not follow this path, or it does not work, then confront the person with someone else present, and if that does not work, with a few more people, like a full-scale intervention (see Matthew 18:15–18). With that kind of confrontation by people who care, we hope there will be an entering into the process outlined above.

If there is not, then there must be some sort of consequence. You let the person know that you will not allow things to continue in the way that they have been and that you are not going to be with them in the same way until they face the problem and deal with it. Then, *you stop seeing them, or limit seeing them in normal ways (like apart from a counselor or a pastor) until they do the process above.* When the process is engaged in, you are on your way to hopeful change. If they do not engage in the process of change, then *you have your answer. It is hopeless.* There is no reason for hope that this person is going to change how he or she is treating you.

So is there reason for you to be hoping? Try the two tests: Are you doing the same thing over and over hoping for different results? If so, try to do something different, like entering this process of change.

Ask yourself: Is there some intervening variable that would make the future different than the past? If not, try to engage the person along the path of change. If that happens, then there is reason for hope.

To successfully navigate the path of change takes more than love or friendly nagging reminders. Here is what God does to start us on the pathway to growth and give us hope for real change.

God starts from a loved position. God does not need the person that he is trying to get to change. His needs are met within the Trinity, and with his other relationships. God always is in relationship and is never alone, so he is not desperate. Make sure that you are also not alone in this process and that you have people who love and support you enough that you do not have to have this person change.

God acts righteously. God is not part of the problem. He does not "repay evil for evil" (Romans 12:17). He does his part of the relationship right. If you have a part in the problem, make sure that you are changing and taking ownership of your own part of things. You cannot demand for the other person to change without changing yourself as well.

God uses others to help. When God wants a person to change, he gets people around that person who can help. Make sure that you use counselors, groups, pastors, or friends to help confront and cure the problem. Don't do it alone without God's ordained delivery system of help: other people.

God accepts reality about the person, grieves his expectations, and forgives. God is not crazy. He faces the reality of who a person is, forgives that person, and then works with the reality of who he or she is. He does not demand perfection when that is clearly not reality. He grieved that on the cross of Jesus. You should give up those perfectionistic standards as well if you are going to be able to work with the problem that faces you.

God gives change a chance. God waits for the change process to work. You might have been waiting a long time, but you have not been working his program. When he gets all of this in place, he is longsuffering, and gives it time. He does not nag. He gives the person a chance to use the help and to change.

God is longsuffering. As we said above, he gives the time to change, and he suffers with it. Sometimes, for a long time. This has two elements that are relevant for you. For God to do this, he must really love someone. For you to make it worth it, you must be sure that the person is someone that you want to go through all of this for. After all, you are not married. You are just dating. Are you sure you want to spend this kind of time and energy? Does it make sense?

And remember, long is not eternal. It is longsuffering, not eternal suffering. It ends at some point when it is clear that the person is not using what is being given to her to help her grow. God withdraws the effort. Not because he is mean, but because it is clear that waiting would not make any more difference.

God separates. God finally leaves the person to his or her own devices and goes away. Maybe this will turn them around. Maybe it won't. But he does prescribe it to us as well when we have tried everything possible. (See Matthew 18:15–18 and 1 Corinthians 5:9–13.) All that is left is for you to stop seeing the person. If he or she changes and comes around later, maybe you can take up the relationship again. But go on your way as if he or she won't. You have no other choice except "crazy hope."

A person you are dating says that he or she "likes you" or "loves you" but is not "in love with you," and wants more time to see where the relationship is going.

What do you do in this situation? Is there a reason for hope? This is a tough one as many people can come along and tell you stories of relationships where a person was slow to come around and then did. So, you keep up the hope that someone you are wanting is going to someday get hit with the bug, see what a great person you are, and fall in love.

First let's look at what you have been doing. Have you been dating in a "just friends" way? If so, you might want to take the relationship to a different level, and treat it more like a dating relationship, keeping certain limits in place. Don't give your heart or your body away, but let the person know that you are interested in taking your relationship past friendship and are wanting to know if there is something more. If you have not done that, then the other person may not even know what you are feeling or wanting.

Perhaps you have let your feelings be known. Some time has passed, but nothing seems to have changed. Now what? You could do one of the following:

Tell him that you have enjoyed your time together, but you are developing more feelings than he is, so you do not see any reason in going forward if it is not mutual. Then end the dating relationship. That way, if he was just taking it easy and not committing because he did not have to, there is a limit that calls for him to either enter into a real relationship with some responsibility or to go away. If you are being used, then the jig is up. If he does change his tune and commit to the relationship, wait awhile before you go back. Give both of you some time to think about it.

End the relationship and don't go back for any reason. Let's say you gave your girlfriend a chance, but she did not have the inclination and feelings necessary to see you as you are and want you. You believe that if she'd wanted you she would have let you know by now. So you end the relationship and move on. In many cases this is the smartest move, because the other person is not going to change. In some cases, it might be premature, but you would have to be dealing with an extremely honest and trustworthy person for that to be true.

Tell him that you are willing to continue if he feels like more time is going to help. But be specific on why you should give it more time. What are the two of you going to do differently, if anything? Why does he feel like more time will help? If he feels like he is in some sort of block, what is he going to do to work through it? Get some sort of reason to continue or some sort of rationale that is behind his wanting to continue. An example would be "I am just off a long-term relationship and it is going to take me some time to trust again." That has reason. "I think this is fun and I would just like to keep going out" is a little less sound if your heart is at stake.

If you are giving the person certain goodies that belong to some sort of commitment more than casual dating, then stop. It is not uncommon for people in an exclusive dating relationship to give up certain boundaries. Calling late at night and wanting to stop by and visit is normal for a "girlfriend-boyfriend" relationship, as is presuming on favors and other things. Some degree of physical affection may also be appropriate in exclusive dating that is not appropriate in "just friends." But if you have been giving of yourself in these ways and then the person plays the "just friends" card, stop doing "more than friends" things. Treat that person as you would any other friend. If she tries to act differently, confront it clearly. If she wants to act like you are dating again, without taking the responsibility for it, don't allow that to happen. If you do, you are probably being used.

Continue with your eyes wide open. This means that you continue to date, wanting things to change, or enjoying it for what it is: a one-sided relationship. But it means that you know that right out front and are taking a huge risk of getting hurt. We think that this is mostly a naïve and risky option, but it has on occasion ended up in something good. (Usually it is because the person in your position began acting differently, like being less codependent.) So, we offer it to you as well. But be warned. You are taking a high-risk chance that your love will go unrequited. Good luck.

These are all examples of not continuing to do the same thing expecting different results. Even the last one is, if you are for the first time facing the reality squarely that there is little hope and taking responsibility for your choice.

The boundaries all have to do with your taking responsibility for reality. You know where the other person stands, and now it is your choice and turn to take control of yourself and do what you think is best. But don't just continue to do the same thing expecting different results, unless there has been some intervening variable. Without one, the past is the best predictor of the future. In our experience, when someone hears the "I love you but am not in love with you" line, it is time to get moving. That usually represents a dependent person who is looking for a relationship to depend on without moving into the position of responsibility that comes with adult love and sexuality. It is fine if the other person has always acted like a friend. But if he or she has been acting like more than friends, and then tells you that you are just friends, our advice is to get moving.

Your dating partner won't commit to the relationship's future.

Do you have hope? Maybe, maybe not. An inability to commit could mean a number of things. It could mean that the person is just not ready for that kind of commitment. He or she might be sure about you, but the timing for engagement is not right. In this kind of scenario you need to ask clarifying questions. Is she sure about you? Why does she think the timing is wrong?

We have seen many people for whom the timing has been wrong. They truly love each other, but are not ready to commit to marriage. For example, they may need to graduate from college or to live on their own for a while. Then, once the timing is right, they get engaged and marry. But their relationship had the firm foundation of certainty in each other's love, and a proven track record of honesty. In other words, they never doubted each other or the relationship. They just wondered about the timing.

In other scenarios, you might be dealing with a commitment-phobic. They love to be in love until it is going to have to cost them some loss of freedom. Should you have hope? Based on what?

If this is the case, and the relationship has gone on for some time, and there is no good reason to not commit other than "I don't want to," and there is no reason to believe that more time is going to allow either one of you to learn more about the other, then what are you basing your hope on?

If, on the other hand, your partner takes ownership of her resistance and says that she has a problem, and will pursue some kind of help to resolve the problem, there may be hope. She is doing something different and there is an intervening variable. If she seeks counseling, for example, or some other kind of help to help get over her fear and resistance, that is a strong show of commitment to the relationship and you might want to honor it by giving more time.

There are some real cases of this where the person is honestly blocked in his ability to go forward, and in humility asks for time and help. This can have a great outcome. But there are also cases where the noncommitted person is so comfortable in the uncommitted relationship that he has no reason to change. This is especially true if sex is involved. The old adage about "why buy the cow when the milk is free" is way too true for a lot of irresponsible people who want the benefits of a relationship without the commitment, costs, and responsibilities. If you are giving away your body, your home, your affection, or other "goodies" of relationship without getting a commitment, then beware. You are being used by a commitment-phobic or commitment-allergic.

At some time, though, when you have exhausted everything, you need to pull the plug. Time has run out, and there is no reason to hope that more time is going to solve anything. Set a limit and stick to it. Give up hope and move on with your life. As Jesus said in the parable of the fig tree, if there is not fruit after giving the tree a lot of effort and time, then cut it down (Luke 13:8–9).

You want a friend to like you in a different way, but it is not happening.

Should you have hope in this scenario? Maybe or maybe not. How long have you been friends? Think of the same test above and apply it. Is there anything different that is going to happen?

Sometimes there is. Friends can have new experiences that cause them to see each other in a different light. There is more exposure and more opening up, a getting closer and being known more and more. Having more knowledge of each other is different and an intervening variable.

So ask yourself if more time is going to do that. Or ask yourself if spending time with each other will help both of you in other ways. I know a couple who were friends for a long time before they became romantically involved with each other. In their case, both were very afraid of dating and of commitment, and the safety that they found in each other healed them both and provided a way to grow into commitment.

In some other cases, someone just needs to break the ice and then allow both persons to see each other in a different light. You might want to tell the friend that you sometimes think of what it would be like to be more than friends, then pursue dating to see what develops. That is open and honest, and sometimes can go to good places.

The problem scenarios are the ones where someone has a crush on a friend and is holding on to hope just for hope's sake. There is no reason to keep on hoping, and in reality the friendship is keeping that person stuck from moving on in his or her life. If you are going to stay, realize that you are hoping that your patience is a new variable in this person's life. Maybe this person has never had someone be patient with him or her before. Or more time might bring more exposure or knowledge.

In a similar vein, bringing it up and talking about it is different also. Or, exploring what dating each other would be like is a different happening as well. But just hoping that a person's feelings are going to change for no good reason other than you want them to would be foolish.

Keep Hope Pure

Remember what God says about hope? First, it is a virtue, and therefore a very good thing. Second, it should be based on reality, or it becomes merely wishful thinking. Third, hope can be distorted and lead to sickness of the heart.

We want you to have hope for your dating life. But we want you to have hope that is based on God, the realities of who you are dating, and the truth of God's principles.

If you are with someone of good character, and your relationship is based on God's leading and sound principles of honesty, communication, vulnerability, humility, love, responsibility, and the like, then there may be good reason for hope.

In addition, we think that there is reason to hope for a good relationship if you are working with God on your own growth. We believe that for the most part healthy people attract and find other healthy people. (We understand that there are exceptions, so don't write us an angry letter if you have not found someone!) Your best chance always depends on your being healthy to attract and be attracted to a good, safe, healthy person. And that has a lot to do with your own commitment to growth and being involved in life. If you are doing that, and involved with God, we think you have great reason for hope in dating.

If you couple that with standing on God's sound principles of growth, you have more reason to hope. Principles like honesty, kindness, firm boundaries, forgiveness, responsibility, faithfulness, and the like will protect you. They are time-tested and proven. God's ways are like a lamp to our feet, and if you follow them, we believe the chances of dating working out well for you are much greater. That is something worth hoping for. As King David observes: "Blessed is the man who does not walk in the counsel of the wicked. . . . But his delight is in the law of the LORD, and on his law he meditates day and night. He is like a tree planted by streams of water, which yields its fruit in season and whose leaf does not wither. Whatever he does prospers" (Psalm 1:1–3).

Hope in God, hope in his principles, hope in people of trustworthy character, and hope in your own growth. Those are truly good reasons for hope. But don't throw hope away on things which have no reality behind them. That kind of hope makes the heart sick.

Take-Away Tips

- Sometimes you need to realize that you are holding on to incompatible wishes. You want something to be true that is not reality, and there is no evidence that it is going to be.
- Good hope is rooted in reality.
- The best predictor of the future, without some intervening variable such as growth, is the past.
- Ask yourself, "What reason has he or she given me to hope that things are going to be different? Is that reason sustainable?"
- Are you seeing evidence of true change and growth? Is there more ownership, a growth path, hunger for change, involvement in some system of change, repentance, or

other fruits of a change of direction? Is there self-motivation for change, or is it all coming from you?

- Are you doing something different in the relationship that could bring about change? Or are you continuing to do the same things expecting different results? If you have not tried something different, there may be some hope if you change.
- Have you changed whatever dysfunction you have been bringing to the relationship?
- Have you followed God's path of being the kind of influence that helps people change? Or are you just wishing and nagging?
- Are you hoping for someone to go deeper who is not going to? Or are you hoping for a noncommitter to commit?
- Is there some reality about a relationship that you need to truly face?
- The best hope is to be involved in God's growth process yourself and pursue good character qualities. The more you are a person of the light, the more you will be able to recognize people who are worth hoping for.
- Ground yourself in values and character. Those are things that do not disappoint.

Chapter 14

Boundaries on Blame

*W*hy do you always . . ."
　　　"Why don't you ever . . ."
"I can't believe you've done it again."
"I don't deserve this kind of treatment."
"This is your fault."
"Who do you think you are?"
"You're so . . ."
"After all I've done for you . . ."

If you have a habit of saying these or similar statements to your date, two things are true: first, they may be true; and second, you are making things worse. These are the results that blaming provides in dating. It has a place, as we will see. But it is less valuable, and more dangerous, than you might think. Let's take a look at setting boundaries on our tendency to blame in dating.

An Honest Legacy

If you struggle with blame, you are not alone. To some extent, it is part of the human condition, and you come by it honestly. Our parents, Adam and Eve, modeled and passed the trait down through the generations: "The woman you put here with me—she gave me some fruit from the tree, and I ate it. . . . The serpent deceived me, and I ate" (Genesis 3:12–13). They pointed the finger of blame on the Devil, each other, and even God. Even then, blame did not work for them. They stayed on the hot seat. God did not relinquish his righteous stance, but followed through with severe consequences for their disobedience.

Watch children grow in their blaming skills; it is so natural. When they are in trouble, they constantly scan the horizon, seeking someone to blame for their difficulties. "I am in time-out because Mom is mean; the dog ate my homework; Billy made me push him." Given our heritage and makeup, it is no small wonder that we are a species of blamers.

What is blaming? It is ascribing responsibility to someone for a fault. When we accuse another of a problem, we are blaming. Blame is not bad in and of itself. It has a good function. Blame separates out who is truly responsible for what in a problem, so that we are able to know how to solve it. It helps differentiate between what is our fault, and what is another's. For example, your girlfriend may have invited you to a party at which her ex is also attending. She was vague about whether or not he would be there. But you also gave the impression that it wouldn't bother you, which wasn't true. So you have a miserable time at the party. As you blame, you figure out that she was at fault for not being clear. You were at fault for not being honest about your feelings. You both know what your growth tasks are to resolve this kind of issue. Blame helped point the way to the solutions.

However, the blame that kills a good dating relationship is when one person sees herself as blameless and attributes almost all of the problems in the relationship to the other person. This sort of blame is not driven by a desire to ferret out reality in order to come to the truth about a matter. It comes from a much darker place in our hearts. This type of blame is based on a denial of our badness. When we cannot tolerate the reality of our mistakes, or that others might see that reality, we point the finger elsewhere. Blame is one of the gravest problems we face, spiritually and emotionally. It keeps us more concerned about being "good" than about being honest.

The irony is that Christians should be the least blaming people in the world, yet we are often the greatest transgressors. We have a new life of forgiveness and grace. There is no condemnation of our sins because of Jesus' death (Romans 8:1–2). We, of all people, have nothing to fear from accepting responsibility for our badness. Yet self-righteousness, excuses, and condemning others are all too prevalent. The best thing you can do for yourself spiritually as well as in your dating life is to begin learning to accept blame for what is truly yours, and give up blaming for what is not another's fault. Below, we will deal with the negative ways that "bad blaming" can affect your dating life.

Blame: An Obstacle to Intimacy

Blaming has the power to negate the growth of intimacy in a dating relationship. When a couple attempts to become closer and more vulnerable, this involves a great deal of risk. Love cannot develop without risks of the heart. When someone feels continually blamed by his date, he is in a state of judgment. He wants to protect himself from the onslaught of blame. He is in conflict between his desire to open up, and his impulse to withdraw protectively.

Travis and Morgan's relationship is an example here. They had been dating for almost a year and were becoming close. They had recently become safe enough with each other to address problems and conflicts. One of them was Travis's irresponsibility. He would not call when he said he would, or he would show up late for events. This grated against Morgan, who set a high value on responsibility, commitment, and punctuality. She had a legitimate gripe, and talked to Travis several times about her feelings about the problem.

Travis tried to change and become more accountable, but he didn't do a very thorough job of it. The problem continued. As time went on, Morgan began to view most of their relationship in light of his flakiness. When he would have a legitimate emergency and not be able to call, she would say, "There you go again, and now you're making excuses." Or when Morgan would blow up at Travis, she'd justify it by responding, "Well, I get angry easily because I have to put up with your irresponsibility."

Though he really cared for Morgan, Travis gradually began to pull away from her. He did not talk about his feelings and experiences much. He kept things superficial or listened to her. Anything to keep away from the blame. Finally, when he realized that he was dreading driving to her home to pick her up for dates, he knew there was a serious problem. He wanted to look forward to being with her, but he felt shell-shocked all the time. He began to avoid making plans with Morgan.

Happily, the couple did work things out and are successfully married now. Travis began telling Morgan about his fear of her blame, and she began working through it. Strangely enough, though he still isn't perfect, he did become more responsible, too. But this was a couple that almost didn't make it because of blame.

A State of Mind

There is even worse news about blame and dating. You don't even have to verbally blame the other person to ruin the relationship. Blaming can be done inside, in your attitude, without your speaking a word. Blame problems are as much about the state of our mind as they are about what we say to our dates. Our inner thoughts and feelings are as important as our behavior (Matthew 5:28). So the man who says, "At least I don't say what I'm thinking to her when I blame" is not off of God's hook by any stretch of the imagination.

This is true for a couple of reasons. First, blame will affect how you approach your date. If you are continually angry, frustrated, and unforgiving, you will not be able to expose your more relational and deep parts to that person. Second, blame has a way of communicating itself through deeds if the words are not present. Silence, coldness, distance, and sarcasm can do the same damage that words do. So if you are to deal with blame, deal with it as a problem of the heart as well as the tongue.

How It Works

How does blame operate inside the one receiving it? Basically, it is experienced as truth without love, and that always feels like judgment or condemnation. All of us need to hear the truth about our selfishness, sin, or immaturity. For example, the first few times that Morgan told Travis that his undependability hurt and bothered her, she was helping him grow.

However, we cannot ingest truth from someone unless we know we are loved. It is too painful. We feel hated or simply that we are bad people. In fact, even when loving people tell us truth it still hurts. A friend of mine (Dr. Townsend's) recently underwent surgery. He had told me about it because he wanted my support. Afterward, he told me, "It hurt me that you didn't call me about how the surgery went." He is a long-term and close friend. He told me this in a straightforward but loving way. And I still felt really bad, in two ways. I felt the sadness and remorse

we are supposed to feel when we realize we have wronged someone (2 Corinthians 7:10–11). And I also felt the "I am all bad"
feelings that indicated that I am not finished in my ability to
receive truth about myself. It only lasted a short while, much
shorter than when I began getting involved in spiritual growth.
But it was long enough to feel the sting.

The point is, if this is what truth feels like when we are safe
and loved, how much worse is it when we are not? We experience deep wrath, either at ourselves or the other person, for that
is the essence of what law without grace brings (Romans 4:15).
So the only way to hear truth is in an atmosphere of love (Ephesians 4:15); otherwise, the "blamee" is placed in a state of condemnation that he must fight either by lashing out at you or at
himself.

Dating: A Petri Dish for Blame

By its very nature, dating is a rich source of blame. People
find themselves pointing the finger at the same person who, a
few months ago, was their ideal soul mate. There are several reasons for this.

The Exploratory Nature of Dating

Your relationship is not a permanent one yet, though it may
be moving that way. But until you wed, there are few prohibi-
tions against your leaving the relationship if you are unhappy
with it. This also means that you don't have to put up with as
much trouble in dating as you do if you are married. If the good
is not worth the bad, you can leave. In marriage, the covenant
is much deeper than deciding whether to stay or go based on any
good-bad ratio. It is for life.

When you do not have to live with someone's faults, you are
less prone to do the hard work of seeing your part in trigger-
ing them. A wife might notice that her covert withdrawal pro-

vokes the rage of her husband. She has seen the dance they do a hundred times, and she knows the only way it will resolve is for her to figure out what she needs to change. But a date can say, "I don't do rage" and exit. This creates more of an opportunity to think it is all him, and none her. This is not to diminish the gravity of the raging man's issue. But it perpetuates the likelihood that she will continue searching for an ideal mate who has no issues, and that she will miss dealing with her own.

Blaming as a Character Trait

We all blame to some extent. However, some people have more of a tendency to blame than others. If you find yourself continually obsessing over your date's faults, you may be one of those people who struggle with blame as part of your character weakness. Blaming isn't better or worse than other character flaws—such as selfishness, impulsiveness, or passivity—but it is certainly significant.

If you have this trait, it may tend to emerge more in the dating arena. Since you are in the process of investigating and evaluating the styles and behaviors of people you date, this process can easily contribute to your blaming weakness. You become a judge without the credentials. If this is your situation, you need to work on some of the tasks at the end of this chapter so that your dating relationship isn't compromised by your blaming tendencies. Until you do some work on this, however, being a blamer in the dating world is a little like letting an active alcoholic tend bar: it is too much temptation for the weaker parts of your nature.

The Romantic Intensity of Dating

Romance is the one quality that distinguishes dating from friendship. Romance carries a great deal of passion and emotional intensity with it. This intensity can have a regressive quality to it. Its depth and strength can tap into old needs and desires from when we were children. That is why people sometimes act silly when they are in love. They feel like kids again, with all the highs and lows that children feel.

During the low part of the childlike swings, blame can take hold. People who have unresolved hurts may unwittingly blame their date for things they aren't guilty of. Their child parts are not able to differentiate between significant formative relationships and the date. The blame strikes the wrong target. That is why many dates have had the experience of "Why is she so mad at me? This punishment is far worse than the offense." It is, more likely, that the romantic fires have unearthed early parts of her soul that never grew up.

If you have experienced this, you will need to do some work on bringing these early hurt parts to some healing, supportive relationships. As you repair these parts in God's process of growth and meet those needs through other caring relationships, you are less likely to feel the intense need to blame your date.

The Results of Blame

Ultimately, blame is its own and only reward. There is a very sick satisfaction that comes in pointing the judgment finger at another. It provides us with the delusion that we are better than we are, and that our biggest problems in life are the sins of other people. It prevents us from seeing our profound need for the grace and mercy of God.

It helps to know how little blame accomplishes, as a way to let go of it. Here are the real results of a dating relationship typified by blame:

- The couple invests more deeply in grievances than in loving.

- One person fights off the blame while the other hunts her down.
- One person idealizes someone he isn't dating, thinking she would never be as bad as who he has now.
- Couples develop unsatisfying ways of solving conflict.
- One person gets labeled as the bad guy and forever has to live with it.
- The good guy is the object of resentment and hurt, as it is hard to be in relationship with a blamer.

The list could go on. It's enough to say, however, that whatever happiness, safety, security, and love you have dreamed of will probably be compromised to the extent that you blame.

Dating and Moral Superiority

Another way that blame can kill a dating relationship is that the injured person can take on an attitude of moral superiority to her offender. She will be shocked and saddened by his behavior, and think, *I would never be capable of the hurt that he has caused.* While it may be true that he has hurt her deeply, she doesn't know the dark capabilities of her own heart (Romans 3:10–18).

Blamers are people who tend to take a victim stance. They feel helpless and run over by powerful people, and they do not see themselves as having much say-so in relationships. This is a child position, and therefore brings with it a sense of innocence. The result is that the blamer—who sees herself as an innocent victim—will forever hold the problem over the offender's head.

It is very hard for dating to survive this problem. The offender will try and try to get in his girlfriend's good graces, but will come back feeling one-down and inferior to his innocently hurt date. Though he needs to own what hurt he has caused, it is very difficult to do so with someone who sees themselves as angel and him as a devil. He will eventually give up trying to do the impossible.

If you tend toward the morally superior position, look at it as something that is working against everything you want in life: mutually adult relationships, personal growth, and freedom. Begin realizing how capable we all are to sin and being hurtful. Actually, it is a relief to get away from a demand to be innocent. Living in reality is less work than living in a fantasy land.

Curing Blame

Many times, a date will feel she has a right to stay frustrated with her boyfriend because he has truly done things wrong. She doesn't want to ignore the issue. So she is in a dilemma: either pretend it's a nonissue, and watch things get worse, or say something, and get labeled as a judge. Neither of these are good solutions, and certainly help no one move toward a successful long-term relationship. Here are some guidelines to curing the blame problem.

Become Self-Scrutinizing

The most important solution is to actively observe your own soul for faults and weaknesses. Blame problems tend to lessen when we are pointing the finger at ourselves first. Remember that you can't give judgment and expect to receive mercy at God's hands: "because judgment without mercy will be shown to anyone who has not been merciful. Mercy triumphs over judgment" (James 2:13). We have won most of the battle when we are much more concerned about our own sins than about the sins of our date.

Your date needs to hear the truth about his failings. But he also needs to first hear about yours. This sets a tone of moral equality that makes things safe. Remember that the ground is always level at the foot of the cross.

Relate to Both the Good and Bad of Your Date

It is hard to maintain a blaming stance if you keep the good parts of your date in mind as much as you do the bad parts. This is not denial; it is relating to the whole person. In fact, chronic blaming is closer to denial, because it can negate your gratitude, appreciation, and love for her good parts. In healthy relationships, people accept the good and bad in each other. They love and hate each other. But love dominates over hate and is the glue that helps us tolerate the bad things that we should not ignore.

Set Boundaries Instead of Blaming

Many times, people blame because they feel powerless and helpless in the relationship. They blame because it is the only way they can protest what the other person is doing. However, there is a better way. It is much more helpful to confront your date in love, let him know what you will not tolerate, and set limits if the behavior continues. That opens you up to having choices, some freedom and power, and you don't feel as controlled by the other person. For example, Morgan could have said to Travis, "I am not going to nag you anymore about not calling me. But that's not how I want to be treated. So the next time you promise to call and don't, I don't want us to see each other for a couple of weeks. I want to be with you, but not the way things are right now." She would have accomplished more this way than with the blaming. Blaming never really solves the problem you have. Limits often do, and thus eliminate the need for blaming in the first place.

Forgive

Another reason people continually blame is that they have difficulty forgiving their date. Forgiveness is canceling a debt that someone owes. We all need forgiveness at times, and we all owe it to each other. Many times, we don't forgive because we feel it's unfair, or we think they are getting away with something. That is why we have a Savior, because the alternative is worse. The problem of being unable to forgive is a real one. To resolve it, it is important to remember that we have a Savior who has forgiven us at the deepest level, and who requires us to let go of the demand for revenge or perfect justice (Matthew 6:12–15), just as he did for us. Let go of the offense, and the need for revenge or perfect justice. Set limits on what can change. Forgive what will not. And evaluate if the relationship is one you want based on those two aspects.

Grieve

While forgiveness is objective in nature, grief is its emotional component. When we cancel a debt, we are letting go of the right to demand revenge. That letting go brings loss and a feeling of sadness. That is the essence of grief. Blamers are angry, but it is the kind of anger that solves no problems. Anger must ultimately give way to grief and sadness. This means you are saying, "I lost," because that is the truth. You may have lost a battle for her to change, or to see things your way, or to understand just how much she hurt you. Stop fighting battles that are not worth winning, or not possible to win. That is what God does every day. He lets go and feels sad about how we choose to conduct our lives (Matthew 23:37).

These steps involve some work, but they will effectively set limits on the negative power of blame in your relationship.

Take-Away Tips

- Learn to humbly listen to correction and restrain the urge to react in blame.
- Use blame as a signal to see if you are afraid, feel judged, or are sad about a fault.

- Take a strong stance of being more concerned about your own soul's state than that of your date's.
- Accept what is negative about your date and work with the realities instead of staying locked in protest, argument, and blame.
- Ask those you trust to let you know when you play the blame game.
- Be a forgiver, and make mutual forgiveness a part of the culture of your dating relationship.

Part Four

Solving Dating Problems: When Your Date Is the Problem

Chapter 15

Say No to Disrespect

C indy had been divorced for two years, and finally felt ready
to reenter the dating world. She met Craig, and the two hit
it off. He was smart and attentive. One thing Cindy was very
drawn to in Craig was that he was able to relate to her as a
woman. Her first husband had been sort of a man's man, and
she had felt worlds apart from him. But Craig was at ease with
her and could talk about emotions and the deeper issues of life
as one who understood. Not only that, but he didn't mind being
with Cindy's girlfriends, either. There was none of that chauvin-
istic distance that some men possess.

He did have a problem though. She noticed it the first time
when they were out on a date at a nice downtown restaurant. She
was flattered by the atmosphere, and felt even more drawn to
Craig's attentiveness as they were being seated at their table.
Then the cocktail waitress, a striking blonde, appeared, and asked
if they wanted drinks or appetizers. Craig's face took on a seductive look, and he said, "No thanks, unless you're on the menu."
The waitress smiled awkwardly and left. Cindy was shocked and
hurt. "You really humiliated me with that comment!" she told
Craig. He held up his hands and said, "What are you talking
about? I was just making a joke. Stop overreacting." Confused,

Cindy backed down and tried to adjust her attitude. They spent the rest of the evening together pleasantly.

Cindy put the event out of her mind, until Craig said something strange to one of her girlfriends at a party a couple of weeks later. Liz had been complaining to the couple about her ex-boyfriend. Craig said, "The guy must be nuts to be treating you that way. If I had someone with your looks and brains, I'd be thanking my lucky stars." Again, when Cindy confronted Craig on it, he said, "Can't you let me be myself? I'm just keeping things light."

The rest of the relationship seemed to go so well that Cindy didn't want to jeopardize a lot for a little. But her antennae were out now, and she began taking note of how often Craig flirted with girls with her by his side. The more involved they became, the more it seemed to happen.

When Cindy mentioned the flirting to a friend, the friend told her, "Look at it this way. Maybe it's the only way he can make conversation with a woman. Besides, at least he's doing it in front of you. That must mean he feels committed to you, to not be hiding it." There was enough sense in what her friend said to keep Cindy doubting her feelings. Yet she couldn't make herself simply let it go.

The worst part of it all was Craig's disregard for her discomfort with his flirting. He did not seem to care or understand how difficult it was for her, even if it were true that it was one hundred percent her reaction. Had he shown some concern for her feelings, she would have been less bothered by the flirting itself. And, as she kept observing, Craig's disregard for her feelings did not limit itself to the flirting issue. Over time, he became more and more insistent on his way and opinions, and less caring about hers. Whenever she would bring up the disregard, Craig's answer was always to minimize her viewpoint and protest his innocence.

Cindy met some women who had known Craig in a previous life, and found out that their experiences were similar. Craig could connect with women very well, as long as other women weren't around, and things were okay with the woman he was dating. But when there were conflicts or other women around, he lost the connection with his date.

Cindy began not only confronting Craig's inappropriateness, but she also began taking action. When he would flirt in her presence, she would quietly pick up her purse and go home, leaving him to explain why she had left. She told him, "I won't be there to experience your immaturity and my humiliation, even if you don't think that is what's going on." This finally broke them up. Cindy was heartbroken, as she really liked Craig. But she couldn't see being married to someone who was great when they agreed, but ran over her feelings when they didn't.

Dissing Is a Problem

There's a term used by some groups of American youth called "dissing." It means "disrespecting," and it refers to the practice of gossiping about someone. When you diss someone, you are liable to get into a fight with the person you dissed, as it is considered a lack of respect and a breach of honor. No matter what the person's social standing, dissing is seen as taboo. It indicates some sort of disregard about the rights and character of the other person.

The dating world also has a problem with dissing. More than talking behind someone's back, however, this is the problem of disrespecting one's dating partner. Disrespect is a serious obstacle to closeness, intimacy, and a couple's chances for marital success.

Respect is a necessary element for any couple to grow in love. Each person needs to feel that they are respected by the person they are getting to know. This involves having esteem or regard for all aspects of the other. Respect is different from empathy, though any relationship needs both to be hand-in-hand. Empathy is the ability to feel another's experience, especially painful ones. Respect is the ability to value another's experience. You may not be able to actually empathize with someone, but you can always take a position of respect for them. For example, a guy may restrain himself from pushing his girlfriend sexually for either reason. He may feel deep compassion for the dilemma he is putting her in. Or he may restrain himself because he respects her right to make her own moral decisions. Relationships develop best when both empathy and respect are in place.

When respect is present, the other person feels that he can be free to be who he is. He can be honest, and still feel connected and safe. He doesn't worry that he will be attacked, humiliated, or treated poorly. When respect is absent, many people will find themselves controlled, neglected, or injured by someone who doesn't care about their needs or feelings.

If you desire to be respected, you are not asking to be treated special. Respect is not worship. It has more to do with being treated as you would like to be treated, which is Jesus' Golden Rule (Matthew 7:12). It means things like the following:

- Your opinion is heard and valued.
- Your differences and disagreeing are validated.
- Your choices are esteemed, even the wrong ones.
- Your feelings are regarded.
- When you are wrong, you are confronted respectfully, not talked down to nor babied.

Craig had a couple of disrespect problems. First, he didn't respect Cindy's need to be treated as special when he was around other women. He laughed off his flirting as harmless, even though the other women were uncomfortable, too. Second, and more importantly, Craig didn't respect Cindy's need to have him consider her feelings when he hurt her. He was so set in his ways that he couldn't see the effect his actions had on her.

How Disrespect Happens

Disrespect flourishes when someone values their own desires above their date's. They may not be actively trying to hurt the other. Instead, the other person's feelings, freedom, or needs get trampled or ignored because of how intent their date is on having their own way. Disrespect tends to be more self-centered than malicious in nature, though that does occur also.

People in dating situations need to know that their feelings, needs, and freedom are respected. When someone is uncomfortable in a sexual situation, or is hurt by a sarcastic remark, or becomes angry with a broken promise, that is a signal that something is going on. The other person needs to take those feelings seriously. The couple needs to talk about what triggered this, and solve the problem.

Disrespect may come out in several ways, and it usually involves some violation of freedom:

- Dominating: The other person won't hear no from her date. When he disagrees, she intimidates, threatens, or rages. She is offended by her date's freedom to choose. For example, a woman may want her boyfriend to spend lots of time with her. When he tells her he'd prefer to do other things, she may disrespect his freedom by becoming angry and telling him their relationship will be jeopardized.
- Withdrawal: One person pulls away when the other exercises some freedom or difference. He may isolate, sulk, or be silent. But he is passively punishing his date

for her differentness. For example, a woman might want to go out with the girls on a night that her boyfriend wants to be with her. While he doesn't complain, he also doesn't call or talk to her for a while. He is showing her that he doesn't respect her freedom.

- Manipulating: One person shows disrespect by subtle stratagems designed to make the other person change his mind. A woman may cry or nag to get her boyfriend to help her paint her apartment when he doesn't have the time.

- Direct violation: The person disrespects by continuing the same hurtful action, even after being asked not to. A man might chronically cancel dates at the last moment. Even though she tells him how much this bothers her, he keeps doing it.

- Minimizing: One person says the other person's negative feelings are simply an overreaction.

- Blaming: When, say, the man talks about the problem, the woman indicates that he himself caused the problem. For example, a man will tell his girlfriend that it hurts when she makes fun of him in public. She might respond with, "If you would pay more attention to me, I wouldn't have to resort to that."

- Rationalizing: The other person denies responsibility for whatever caused the problem. For example, the chronically late date excuses the hurt his girlfriend feels by saying, "I understand your feelings, but it was the freeway traffic, not me."

Respecting someone doesn't mean that you agree with them. Nor does it mean that you will comply with what they want. It means that their feelings matter because those emotions belong to a person who matters. Listen to, understand, and try to help the situation.

Margaret was dating Mike, who traveled a lot in his business. As they were getting more involved, she began wanting more contact with him, which made sense. She wanted Mike to call her every night when he was traveling. This was very difficult, if not impossible, for him, because of flying times and meeting schedules. He tried to call Margaret. When he didn't, she would get very hurt and feel unloved. He would try harder, but it wouldn't work. Finally, he told her, "I really care about your feelings, but I can only do so much. Can we work this out another way?" She thought about it and realized he wasn't the problem. She had suffered from abandonment issues all her life with a dad who had moved away. She realized she was putting her abandonment on him, and began to let go of her dad at the same time. Margaret agreed that if Mike could call, that would be enough. Mike respected her feelings, but the couple used the information to solve the real issue.

If your feelings, time, opinion, or values are not being respected, you need to take some sort of action. You may need to end your silence and bring up the issue. You may need to bring it up as a serious issue, not to be put off. You may need to set consequences on the event happening again. I knew a woman whose date was always having fun at her expense when they went out with friends. Finally, she started driving a separate car to the events so that she could leave when he got disrespectful. It took only a few occurrences of this for him to see that she was serious, and things got better.

The Progression of Disrespect

We aren't born respecting others. Instead, we begin life highly concerned with our own lives and hardly aware of the needs of others. As we mature, however, others come into the picture more. Over time, we are supposed to learn that others' needs and feelings are important. But this is a learned ability, not an innate one.

Sometimes a person will date someone who seems very respectful at first. They listen, acknowledge the other's opinions, and will often defer to them. Then, as the couple gets more comfortable, the respect seems to dissipate, and the other person feels devalued or put down. The hurt person will often wonder, *How did he lose the respect he had for my feelings? Did familiarity breed contempt?*

The reality is different. Respectful people don't lose respect over time, they increase it. As the relationship deepens, they are connected with that much more of the person, and respect those additional parts of the person. They may become more comfortable and casual, but they still care about the feelings of the other person. This is a character trait. It is stable and is not dependent on situations. So people who seem to stop respecting you over time, in all likelihood, *have never had true respect for others' needs and feelings.* They may be socialized on the outside, knowing etiquette and the rules of society, but their heart is still bent on getting their way. So if you notice disrespect increasing, you are probably instead seeing something that was hidden beginning to manifest itself.

Saying and Doing

Another important aspect of noticing disrespect is that it is about what we do, not what we say we will do. Anyone can apologize and say they will change. That takes a certain amount of character growth, but not as much as actually changing and doing what we promise. For example, the man who chronically broke dates at the last moment might really listen to how much this hurt his girlfriend. He might apologize profusely. And he might promise that he will, from this day forward, follow through on his commitments. Yet he still tends to overcommit to things and have to back out. It is not disrespectful to fail. It is, however, disrespectful to continually fail in an area that hurts another, and not take steps to resolve the failure. Don't condone disrespect in word or deed.

What Does Not Cure Disrespect

A disrespectful relationship has ultimately to do with character. Disrespect can be caused by selfishness, control, lack of understanding, and other things. Here are some things that will not cure a pattern of disrespect.

Ending the Relationship Immediately

So many people who have difficulty setting limits will simply walk away from the relationship when they encounter disrespect. Almost out of the blue, they will terminate things, citing that they won't put up with disrespect anymore. This is a sad and unhelpful way to solve the problem. There is much you can do, as we will show, before having to end things. *Dating should be an arena in which you solve problems while in the relationship, rather than ending the relationship when you experience problems.* Premature endings don't bode well for your future marriage years, either, or any type of relationship. Learn to deal with disrespect before you end things.

Compliance

Attempting to please a disrespectful date is pretty futile. While compliance may seem to calm down the battle, it cannot win the war. Disrespect has self-centeredness at its core. Compliance creates the illusion that disrespect has no consequences, so the selfishness remains, or can even get worse.

We are all called to love others, even the disrespectful: "This is my command: love each other" (John 15:17). But love is not compliance. While loving someone means taking a stance for

their best, compliance rescues them from the consequences of
their sin and immaturity. For example, suppose you are dating
someone who has a hot temper. When he gets angry, he gets
mean and critical with you, disrespecting your need for safety
and security. You may comply with his rages, calming him down
and taking responsibility for his anger. This may soothe him temporarily, but it will not cure the character problem with which
he is struggling: "A hot-tempered man must pay the penalty;
if you rescue him, you will have to do it again" (Proverbs 19:19).
A good source for more information on compliance with disrespect is our book *Boundaries*.

Retaliation

It is perfectly natural to want to meet disrespect with disrespect. If she dates around on you, then you date around on her.
Let her see what it feels like. The problem is, what is natural
is often not what is mature. We are, by nature, revengeful legal-
ists: an eye for an eye. Yet retaliation is ultimately ineffective.
That is why God sent Jesus—the law failed to make us righteous
people. When you take revenge, you tend to receive either a
grudging compliance from the other person, or escalation of the
disrespect. Neither one touches the heart of the person or the
issue. Leave retaliation demands nailed to the cross of Christ:
"If it is possible, as far as it depends on you, live at peace with
everyone" (Romans 12:18).

Complaining without Consequences

As we stated in our parenting book, *Boundaries with Kids*,
setting boundaries without setting consequences is a form of
nagging. The disrespecter learns that his greatest problem is not
the hurtfulness of his behavior, but only the annoyance of your
complaining. There is very little motivation to grow and change.
Cindy, who at the beginning of the chapter struggled with the

flirtatious Craig, simply protested to him about his behavior. Yet it was much later that she finally set the limits of going home when he was inappropriate. They did break up, but at least the consequence did force some sort of change. Had she only protested to Craig, who knows how long they would have been in this stalemate? If you complain about disrespect and set a limit, be prepared to also establish a consequence to back up your words.

What Does Cure Disrespect

Finally, if you are experiencing a disrespectful dating relationship, here are a few action points which can go a long way to resolve it.

Don't Wait to Deal with It

As we mentioned, much of the time, disrespect is a character problem. One aspect of character problems is that they don't simply resolve over time. They need interventions of truth and grace to work out. The longer you wait to address disrespect, the more you can expect it. Require respect today, and you have a better chance of it: "making the most of every opportunity, because the days are evil" (Ephesians 5:16). This doesn't mean setting out some abrupt rule book on the first date. It does, however, mean that when your date ignores your request to get you home by a particular time because he is having so much fun, that you address the problem then and there.

Get to Know Your Date in the Context of Other Relationships

Sometimes you may wonder if you are just overreacting and being too sensitive. For example, your girlfriend may be inconsistent in when she says she will be somewhere, and you find yourself waiting around forever for her. Yet she may say you're being picky and controlling. This may be true. So get around her and her friends and family. Find out what those who know her say about her habits. They may say she's never been flaky. Then again, they may say she has no concept of time, and it drives them crazy too. This isn't spying. It is how people get to know someone. Dating should not be done in a vacuum.

Say No

A simple test of disrespect is to disagree about a preference and see what happens. A respectful person will listen, negotiate, and come to some sort of mutual compromise. A disrespecter will find some way to change the no to a yes.

Address the Disrespect as a Problem

Mention to the person that you feel controlled, dismissed, or unheard about this area. Let them know it hurts and distances you. Some people disrespect out of ignorance. They dominate because no one has set enough limits with them, but they are also goodhearted folks. If you address your feelings to the ignorant person, he will most likely want to change, because he is invested in the relationship, not in controlling you. However, some people disrespect because they care more about themselves than they do the relationship. When you bring your feelings to them, they are likely to rationalize, deny, or blame— anything but change. This is a major red flag.

Clarify

Be very clear and specific about several aspects of the problem:

- What bothers you about the disrespectful behavior: *You dismiss my opinions when we talk about issues.*
- What feelings it brings up in you: *I feel hurt and distanced.*

- How you would like to be treated: *Give us both equal time and respect when we discuss a topic.*
- What you will do if things do not change: *I will probably not see you for a while, until you are able to see that this is a severe problem.*

Bring Others In

Don't do this alone. Get support, feedback, and reality testing from safe friends. Disrespect can evoke certain childlike parts of our nature which long to please hurtful people in order to get their love. If we have childhood hurts in which we attempted to repair distant or critical parents, we are at risk for being trapped by disrespect. That is why some people put up with the most disrespectful relationships imaginable. Being around healthy people can help you be free to address the problem.

Own Your Own Part

Remember that you might be making disrespect easier, and take the plank out of your own eye before removing your date's speck (Matthew 7:3–5). Your part may be several things:

- Not saying anything, which can imply consent
- Treating it lightly or as something cute or funny in your date
- Vacillating between doing nothing and having rage fits about it, which conveys a confusing message
- Making it all your fault and problem instead of your date's

Take ownership of the issue. Change what you need to change. But require that your date treat you respectfully. In our experience, when you do this, one of two things tends to happen: you get more respect from those who have it to give; and you get left by those who don't have it. Both results are good ones.

Take-Away Tips

- Respect and esteem your date's thoughts, feelings, and choices; require that sort of treatment from him.
- Address disrespect early in the relationship. If you feel disrespected and aren't sure it is really going on, ask your date and get the dialogue started.
- Make a distinction between differences and disrespect. You can disagree and even get angry with each other respectfully.
- Avoid the tendency to overlook disrespect, hoping it will get better over time. Start seeing if it is curable.
- Don't fight fire with fire. Start with vulnerability and state your desire for the relationship to be better.
- See if you are making it easier to be disrespected by putting yourself in the one-down position in the relationship.

Chapter 16

Nip It in the Bud

I don't understand what happened," Todd told me (Dr. Cloud). "It seemed that we were doing so well, and then she just came in one day and told me that she didn't want to be with me anymore. She was very angry about a lot of things."

"Did you have any warning?" I asked. "Did she give any signs?"

"Well, sometimes I could tell that she was sort of pouty about things. There would be things I did that she would not like, but I never thought it was a big deal. Like when I would be late, or go out with my friends without telling her. Or sometimes, I would cancel on her to go play basketball if a good game came up. That kind of thing. But I never thought it was a big deal," he mused.

"Sounds like it was a bigger deal than you saw," I said.

Then I heard Mary's side of things. It was a little different to be sure.

"I got to a place where I just couldn't stand it anymore. He was so inconsiderate," she began. "He would just not show up for things we had planned. I asked him to let me know, but he never would. He would always have a reason like 'The game just got put together,' or something like that. It was never his fault, but he chose his sports over me."

"Did you tell him?" I asked.

"I tried a few times, but he really wasn't listening. And it never made a difference in his behavior. He just would do pretty much what he wanted to do, and I was supposed to be fine with it."

"Did you ever try to give him any kind of boundaries?" I asked.

"Like what?" she asked me in return.

"Like tell him that if he were not on time or did not keep the date, he could forget getting together that night, or that week. You would make some plans that you could depend on," I asked.

"That seems really mean," she said. "I could never do anything like that. It is too harsh."

I did not tell her that it seemed a lot less harsh than a sudden breakup without any warning.

The issue in Mary and Todd's relationship was not an uncommon one. There is a person in the relationship who is probably not that bad a person. But he (Todd in this case) or she is and always has been allowed to get away with certain character patterns of taking advantage of other people's niceness and not being responsible to the relationship. Usually, there is a pattern of inconsiderateness.

In dating, this can be the kind of thing that Mary dealt with. Or it can be physical pressure, or attitudes, or any other way that one person hurts another short of something evil. And the formula that Mary did not know is this: *In relationships, you get what you tolerate.* Why, we are not sure. In part it is because people who allow people to get away with things seem to attract the kind that would want to get away with less-than-considerate behavior. Another reason seems to be that whenever we do not have good limits with each other, there is a regression on the part of the person who is enabled to be less than mature.

In any case, you can bet that for the most part, especially in the world of dating, *you will get what you tolerate.* And if you are like Mary, you will get enough of it that you cannot tolerate anymore, and then you will be alone again.

A Better Way

We think that there is a better way. Set your limits early on. Make them clear. Enforce them and stick to them. In short, nip it—whatever the problem is—in the bud and do not allow that weed to grow in the garden of your relationship.

If you are someone who allows yourself to be treated in a certain way in the beginning of a relationship, you are allowing certain things to get a foothold in the relationship and they will grow. There are two dangers to this. One, if the person is someone you will grow to love, you don't want those dynamics present in the relationship at all. Second, if the person is not someone you will love, then you want to have them run into those limits and go away sooner rather than later. It is always better to "nip it in the bud."

This is similar to the idea we talked about in "Adapt Now, Pay Later," but there we talked a lot about being who you truly are early on. And we talked a bit about setting limits. Here we want to remind you that you need to set the tone early in how you expect to be treated so that the person knows that he or she is dealing with someone who has self-respect and will not tolerate being treated poorly. This will weed out selfish people, and discipline sloppy ones. Both are good things to do.

Some Weeds Worth Confronting

Proverbs says that it is a good thing to overlook an offense: "A man's wisdom gives him patience; it is to his glory to overlook an offense" (Proverbs 19:11). Patience and the ability to overlook some offenses are wonderful qualities. No one wants to be around a person who is quarrelsome and makes an issue out of everything that goes wrong. "Chill out" is an expression made for such persons.

But overlooking certain negative character patterns long-term can lead to a real problem. Here are some things, and there are certainly more, that should not be tolerated for very long:

- Being inconsiderate regarding time or commitments
- Not following through on promises or commitments
- Disrespectful comments that are degrading or otherwise hurtful, alone or in front of others
- Pushing for physical relationship past where you allow
- Unfair or irresponsible financial dealings, such as presuming on your generosity or patience
- Critical attitudes
- Other consistent ways of hurting your feelings that are clearly his or her fault and not your own sensitivities
- Controlling behavior

These are not too far from the kinds of things that you can't live with, but some are also part of the things that are in between those and being considerate. To be sure, you would not want to live with them for long. And if you learn to nip it early, and have consequences to back up what you are saying, you won't have to. But nagging will never do. Set your limits and stick to them. Tell the person that you won't tolerate certain things and if they continue, he or she cannot see you until they learn how to not act that way. This is another advantage of doing this early. You don't yet have a lot to lose.

Remember, we are not talking about sending the person away after one small offense. If you are like that, he or she would do well to have some limits with you! Remember, it is a glory to not make an issue out of everything. But, if it is significant, and if it is a pattern, then deal with it early. You will be glad you did.

Short Accounts

The best accounts are short ones. As Ephesians 4:25–27 says, "Therefore each of you must put off falsehood and speak truthfully to his neighbor, for we are all members of one body. 'In your anger do not sin.' Do not let the sun go down while you are still angry, and do not give the devil a foothold."

The truth of saying what bothers you is the best policy. But say it in love without sinning yourself. Do not return evil for evil. Have grace and love in your expression of what you don't like, but do it honestly and quickly. Don't let the sun go down on it. In other words, don't cover it up in the darkness. Instead, deal with it that day if possible. If you don't, evil will have an opportunity to work in your relationship, either through enabling it to continue, or resentment and bitterness. Be loving, but tell the truth.

We cannot tell you how much misery could be prevented if people followed this principle. Nip it fast. You will either chase off a bad person, or make sure a good one does not slip into one.

Take-Away Tips

- You will get what you tolerate.
- Don't confront on everything that happens. If you do, you will be quarrelsome and difficult to be around.
- Do confront on things that are important—issues of dignity, consideration, values, and the like. Maybe let a few things slide once or twice, but do not allow a pattern of disrespect to occur.
- When you confront, do it soon, with love and with total honesty.
- If you follow this advice, you will show self-respect, which demands respect from others, and you will get it.
- If you follow this advice, you will save yourself from some very bad people. They will go away early. Or, you will help some pretty good ones to become better. Either way, you win.

Chapter 17

Set Appropriate
Physical Limits

*J*enny and Dave had been dating for a while. They were having fun, spending more and more time together, sharing more thoughts and feelings, and naturally feeling closer. They spent a lot of time together enjoying mutual interests like movies, sports, and spiritual activities. They felt like they were falling in love.

Physically, they were becoming more affectionate also. Hugs were turning into kisses. They enjoyed the closeness, never thinking they would get into trouble. But kisses were turning into more desire. They were both committed to their values of abstinence before marriage. So, always before it got too heated, they would back off. They both felt comfortable with each other.

Their relationship went along for a while like this, until one night they went too far. They had been lying on the floor watching videos and feeling very warm and close. Beginning with innocent affection, they moved on from there.

Jenny felt as if it had happened almost without her. Her values about physical limits before marriage were strong, but that night her values seemed to be somewhere far away from her awareness as she got lost in the closeness with Dave. It was a little like a whirlwind inside her head, and she really wondered in a way how it had happened.

Afterwards, she felt bad, and was remorseful about having given herself away. She had had no intention of going that far. The guilt was pretty strong, but at the same time she felt confused. Very aware of her feelings for Dave, she began to wonder why loving him physically was so wrong. Everything had felt so right, even if it was wrong. Confusion and doubt began to take over in her mind. She felt herself drifting away from him, even as she was drawn closer. Now she was feeling not at all like her old self, and she wondered what to do from there.

Sound familiar?

Okay, let's talk. Here is the issue. You are past thirteen, single, and have a body that is ready for sex. But you are not married. You are probably dating, find yourself in situations where either your partner, yourself, both of you, or just your body is saying, "Go for it." What do you do? How far is too far? Why should you wait? Are you missing out on something good and depriving yourself for no reason? Or is there a good reason to have limits on sexual expression? What will it hurt, you ask yourself, at the same time knowing that something is wrong.

Or, the issue takes on meaning in your dating relationship. Will he still love you if you say no? Or, if you really loved him, wouldn't you say yes? Or, if you are in love, are you missing out on a natural expression that would enhance your closeness?

All of these are very good questions that singles ask, and are the topic of this chapter. Let's take a look.

The Big Rule, and More

If you have hung around the church for very long, you have probably heard that God wants people to reserve sex for marriage. If you haven't and that is news to you, then I can understand the shock you might be feeling. For many people, both inside and outside of the church, it does not make sense. If it feels so good, and is good for the relationship, and both people are consenting, then what is the problem?

For many people sexual abstinence is just a religious rule that makes no sense. But for others, it has real value from their experience in dating and the single life. They have reaped the consequences of pain that sex out of the commitment of marriage can bring. They feel that there are good reasons to wait. And as clinicians who have worked with many of those who have made such a decision, we agree. So, let's see why.

First of all, let's see what the rule is, and then let's talk about it in the context of dating. Here it is:

> It is God's will that you should be sanctified: that you should avoid sexual immorality; that each of you should learn to control his own body in a way that is holy and honorable, not in passionate lust like the heathen, who do not know God; and that in this matter no one should wrong his brother or take advantage of him. The Lord will punish men for all such sins, as we have already told you and warned you. For God did not call us to be impure, but to live a holy life. Therefore, he who rejects this instruction does not reject man but God, who gives you his Holy Spirit. (1 Thessalonians 4:3–8)

In this passage is not only the rule, but the reasons as well. Let's look at them one by one.

Holy and Honorable

Okay, so you don't want to wear a white robe and be a holy person. But there is more to holiness and honor than that. Basically, holiness means purity and to be set aside for a high purpose. Honor means that something has great weight. Literally, when I looked up the Greek word used here for honor it means things like "dignity, precious, of high price or value, or high esteem." Basically, God is not saying for you to become a weird person roaming in the desert who is not romantic or sexual or passionate. He loves those things. He created them. He wants you to have them, and he is very much like that himself.

But what he begins with saying here is that sex is not a casual thing. It is holy, set apart for a high purpose, and has *great value, dignity, and esteem*. In fact, it is the highest form of expression that you can give another person of your romantic love for him. It is the highest value that your body possesses to give to someone you are in a romantic relationship with. And, for that reason, like other things of high value, to spend it casually or unwisely is foolish, and you will be cheated in the end. You will have spent all that you have, and maybe have nothing to show for it after the music has died.

Amanda felt that way when she and Monte broke up. She had thought that he was "the one." He had seemed that way to her, and they had talked a lot about being together forever. She was sure that he loved her, and he talked about one day getting engaged, "when he was really ready." What that meant for him was when his career was a little more settled down. He wanted to be stable in his profession before he got married and wanted to wait. It sounded good to her. She knew that she loved him.

But he did not want to wait for sex. Marriage and commitment could be in the future, but why should they wait to enjoy each other? So they began sleeping together. After all, they would one day get married.

But, as this common story goes, Monte decided later that he just did not see marriage in his immediate future. In fact, being in a relationship at that time in his life was beginning to feel too confining to him as well. So they broke up.

Amanda was devastated. She felt as if her heart was ripped out of her. This, to her, was not just a breakup. It was more than that. She felt as if she had lost a part of herself when Monte left.

She thought they would be together forever and she had given all of herself to him. So she felt as if a lot of herself went away as well. In short, she had spent it all, and was left with nothing to show for giving herself away. She felt cheated, empty, and betrayed.

In contrast, I talked to a man recently who had also "found the one." They were headed for marriage. But, having had a few experiences like Amanda, he had decided to wait. They were planning to get married later in the year.

As things began to get more serious, this man's girlfriend also decided that marriage was not for her at that time in her life. So she broke up with him. He was grieved, as he loved her and wanted to be with her. But, in contrast to other times in his life, he was not broken. He was able to go through the missing in a different way than he had before. Part of the reason he was able to move on with his heart intact was because of his decision to not have sex. It was as if he had held on to himself until it was safe to let go, and since it never was safe, he had lost her, but he still had himself intact. He felt more whole, and like he had more integrity. Why? Because sex and the heart are connected.

What is the first lesson here? It is that sex is set apart for a purpose, and has great value. It is for lifelong commitment and needs to be esteemed. In a physical and spiritual sense, *it is all you can give someone.* Therefore, it should not be given away lightly. In the same way that you do not give your life away to anyone but the person you marry, so your body should belong only to the person you marry as well. *It is all you have.* Don't throw it away. Give it to someone who is going to give himself to you forever.

Self-Control

Josh had made a commitment to wait on sex. Then he started dating Marty. Fun-loving and spontaneous, smart and full of life, she was getting his attention. In fact, what he liked most about her was how full of life she seemed, and the way that she went after life itself.

He liked her free-spirited nature, but when it came to the physical, she wanted to go further than he felt comfortable with. He would stop their interactions, and she would try to continue. He would tell her no and she would first get coy and flirtatious, and then push harder. When he said no to that, she would either get annoyed at him, or hurt, and pout.

He tried to talk to her and she would say, "What's the big deal? Why can't we have a little fun? It's okay if we like each other." He talked to her about his spiritual commitment and what he believed about sex, and she said she agreed, but still thought it was okay if you really liked someone. He did not quite understand her thinking.

Then he began to notice something. In other areas of their relationship she did the same thing. When he would want to do something different than she wanted, she had a difficult time respecting his wishes. He did not want to have total control, he just wanted some mutual give-and-take. And it seemed that things were only okay with her if they were what she wanted as well. She had a difficult time doing what he wanted if it wasn't her first choice.

Finally, although he loved her "going for it" attitude, he realized that she was unable to be happy if she was not getting her own way, and sex was just a sign of an overall character issue that she had in delaying gratification. He loved her gusto for life, but it was beginning to look self-serving. It saddened him to see, but he was being honest with himself. He could not continue with someone who could not respect his choices and the word *no*.

Like Josh was realizing, self-control has serious implications for your life. As Paul says, "Each of you should learn to control his own body" (1 Thessalonians 4:4). Why is that important?

Basically it is a sign to you that a person is capable of delay of gratification and self-control, which are prerequisites of the ability to love. If someone cannot delay gratification and control himself or herself in this area, what makes you think that they can delay their own gratification in other areas of sacrifice for you? What is going to curb the "I want what I want now" mentality in the rest of life? If someone is able to respect the limit of hearing no for sex, then that is a character sign of someone who can say no to their own desires and hungers in order to serve a higher purpose, or to love another person.

You fall in love with a person and think about making a real, committed relationship with him or her. Naturally, that is going to mean some sacrifice down the road. You are going to want to be with a person who can deny himself or herself for the sake of the relationship in many areas. Think of the areas of sacrifice that a relationship takes. There are sacrifices of time, when you might want to spend time on your favorite hobby, and yet the family needs you. There are sacrifices of money. One person may want to buy a new car, and yet the family needs money for the home. There are sacrifices of getting one's way. One person may want to go to one place for dinner and the others want something different.

And then most importantly, there is the sacrifice that it takes to work out conflict. One person is hurt and wants to strike back in anger or hurt, yet to reconcile, the ability to put one's own desires aside for the sake of the relationship is necessary. If someone does not have self-control and delay of gratification in pleasure, can they delay the gratification of getting his or her own way in conflict?

Think about it. You want to be with a person who can hear and respect the no of others. Having a boundary in sex while you are dating is a very important test to see if the person loves you. We have all heard people refer to the line "If you love me, you will." In reality, you should say back, "If you love me, you won't make demands that I do not feel comfortable with." Love waits and respects, but lust must have what it wants now. Are you being loved, or are you an object of self-serving lust? Saying no is the only way to know.

We cannot overemphasize the value of your picking a person who has the ability to delay their own gratification. If you are with someone who ultimately has to have what they want when they want it, you are in for a long time of misery. Choose someone who can delay gratification for the sake of you and the relationship. To the extent that he or she says "I must have what I want now," you are in trouble. Boundaries with sex are a sure-fire test to know if someone loves you for you.

Passionate Lust

Paul also teaches against passionate lust (1 Thessalonians 4:5). What does that mean? Does it mean that God wants you to not be a passionate person with strong desires? Not at all. In fact, he himself has a passionate desire for you. The meaning here is a lust for that which is forbidden outside of marriage. Why is that important?

Basically, a healthy person is someone who is integrated. What that means is that all aspects of a person are connected and working together. Sex is connected to love, relationship, and commitment. The body, the soul, and the mind are all working together. Like we said above, the body is given 100 percent to someone who gives you 100 percent of everything else. If someone has not married you, then they have given less than 100 percent, so they get less than 100 percent of your body. With the way that some people treat the people they are dating, they would be lucky to get a kiss once a month, much less casual sex! We have heard so many stories of people being used for sex when there is absolutely no intent by the person to make a commitment. Yet 100 percent of the body is taken.

This is a very disintegrating way to live, and if you are giving yourself to someone who is a luster and not a lover, you are headed for trouble. "Lusters" are people who have divided souls, and do not develop the deeper aspects of themselves which are necessary for a lasting relationship. Many lusters have sexual addictions that are trying to meet deeper needs that they cannot express in a healthy way.

Janet found this out the hard way. She loved Steve and wanted to be with him. So she gave in to sleeping with him. Even though it was against her values, she liked the fact that he wanted her so desperately. But what she found was that he did not have the ability to connect in other ways. When she would want deep talking, or sharing of feelings, he would withdraw from her. He was unable to be vulnerable on a level of needs or emotions. But when it came to sex, he was all for it.

This is the case with lust. It often occurs in a person who is not developing in other areas of intimacy. Sex during dating often hides a person's lack of relational skills—skills that are going to be needed in marriage. In all the heat and romance of dating and sex, the inabilities in the relational realm are never noticed. Then a person finds himself or herself serious with or marrying a sex addict who is incapable of a real relationship. Instead of *expressing* love through sex, the luster *replaces* love with sex.

Do not allow dating to be a place where you act out lust and avoid relationship. And do not allow it to be a place where you have no boundaries with another person and allow them to do that with you. Remember, for every sex addict, there is someone allowing that person to continue in that pattern. Say no before it is too late and you find yourself with a nonrelational person.

In terms of yourself, sexual abstinence is a great way to find out how fulfilled you are as a person. The reason that you have acted out in a sexual way may well have been to fulfill deep long-ings and hurts that are still unhealed in your soul. There is always a need driving lust, and you do not want to allow that to continue.

Sally was like that. She came into counseling because of her recurring tendency to act out sexually. She wanted to be com-mitted to her spiritual values, but kept finding herself sleeping around. She realized that she was unable to stop.

As we began to explore the issue, I got a commitment from her to get some support that she could call in case of an "emer-gency," and to promise me that she would commit to abstinence so that we could find out what was driving her to this danger-ous behavior. (The risk of HIV is higher than many realize when engaging in promiscuity, and it does not mean anything that the person has passed a test recently. The virus could be in the unde-tectable time period.)

When she was dating, she found that she was especially lured by the attention that guys would give her when they were hit-ting on her. She liked the chase, as it made her feel wanted. As we worked with that, and she began to analyze the drives and the feelings behind the sexuality, she began to see that she was trying to compensate for some deep feelings that she had of not being wanted and desired.

Sally's dad had left the home when she was young, and she had basically grown up without a lot of male attention and affec-tion. When a man would come on to her and pursue her, she felt wanted, and it temporarily took her away from the inner lone-liness and lack of closeness she experienced with her dad. Until she felt it again, and she was driven to another liaison.

When she was dating someone more steadily, it was even tougher to say no. It seemed that she just could not live with the risk of not having a man be attuned to her.

This is an example of a need that drives someone into "sensuality." Ephesians tells us that along with this, there is a "continual lust for more" (Ephesians 4:19). Lust, or uncommitted sex, will never heal the longing in your soul for whatever is driving it. Sally needed some healthy male validation in her life that her father never gave her. As she began to find that in a good support group and in counseling, her sexual addiction went away. She felt more whole, more loved, and more in control of herself. She was also beginning to be more able to pick good men to date. Her addiction was not making her choices for her any longer.

I had one woman I worked with tell me once that she had spent years making decisions about men with her "crotch." As she worked through her underlying needs, she began to make decisions based on her values instead.

Here are some things that drive passionate lust:

- The need for intimacy and connection
- The need for power
- The need to feel admired and desired
- The need to be free and out from under parental control (something many adults are still under)
- The need to avoid working through pain and loss
- The need to overcome shame and bad feelings about oneself

If you are caught up in passionate lust or with someone who is, then chances are that these issues are not being worked out. The lust is keeping you from integrating your soul. Just like a drug addict is not growing when he or she is using drugs, your soul is not growing if you are acting out lust.

That is what passionate lust does. It splits you from your real heart, your mind, your values, and the life that you truly desire. Lust gains momentary pleasure at the expense of lasting gain. You will never find the fulfillment that your soul needs if you let your lust dictate your life and choices. Nor will you find what you need if you give in to the lust of someone else. Giving in to a sex addict (even though the person may not look like one) is giving yourself to someone who is ignoring growth, and the deeper deficits of their own character.

We have listened to countless stories of married women, especially, who gave themselves to someone who could not wait, only to find out later in marriage that the person was incapable of real relationship. Learn from their experience.

Wronging Someone

Paul also teaches that when sex occurs outside of marriage, someone is always wronged. Remember the verse: "In this matter no one should wrong his brother or take advantage of him" (1 Thessalonians 4:6). When someone sleeps with someone whom he or she is not married to, he or she is hurting that person.

Why is that? For all the reasons that we talked about earlier. When people sleep together outside of marriage, here is what is happening to them.

- They are splitting their soul and body. A real division takes place inside of a person that is very difficult to repair for later relationship. The body is given 100 percent, and the soul is only given or connected with to some lesser degree. That requires a split in the person.
- They are taking away a very precious aspect of themselves and someone else which is of great value and esteem, and cheapening it. It becomes casual, of lesser value, and will have less value later with someone they really care about. In a sense, they are making casual or nonlasting people as important as the one they commit to for life.

- They are causing a person to not develop deeper aspects of relatedness and spirituality. They are potentially helping someone to remain shallow, and making certain aspects of the person's soul unavailable for relationship.
- They are coming in between a person and God. God has asked everyone to submit their sexuality to him so that he can develop it and guide it to marriage. Sleeping with someone causes them to disobey God and creates a barrier between them and God.
- They are helping a person deny hurt and pain, thus keeping them stuck in an addictive cycle which sets them up for later trouble.
- They are using them for their own pleasure and lust, and that is a long way from love.
- While they are using them, they are keeping them back from finding someone who will truly value them.
- They are setting them up for heartbreak and devastation if they break up with them and leave them, having taken something so precious.

If you say that you are a person of love, then you won't wrong someone you love. You will wait. You will respect them enough to not push them or use them in this way. And vice versa, do not allow anyone else to wrong you. Love waits to give, but lust can't wait to get.

Accepting God

Finally, Paul teaches us in 1 Thessalonians where the authority for sexuality comes from. Ultimately it does not belong to us. It belongs to God. In a sense, our bodies are not ours, they are his. So, the question gets into a bigger realm than just who someone is going to sleep with or not. It gets into the question of who someone is going to obey or not.

There are few better tests for whether or not someone lives a life in submission to God than what he or she does with their sexuality. Sex is such a powerful and meaningful desire, that to give it up and obey God in that area is a true sign of worship. It is a true sign that someone is willing to say, "Not my will, but Thine be done." And that becomes important for a serious reason later on.

In a long-term relationship, you want to be with a person who knows that they are not God and always places themselves in a position of submitting to God. What if your spouse, for example, is angry and wants to punish you or strike back at you in hurt or revenge? Or is tempted in some area of lust or addiction? Or wants to blow off all responsibility and revert to a carefree teenage life? Or is tempted to avoid paying taxes? If that person is the ruler of his or her own soul, what is going to stop him?

If he or she is a person who, no matter what the temptation is or desire of the flesh, can be counted on to say, "Not my will but Thine," then you are with a safe person. If you can trust him or her to do it God's way, you will always be a beneficiary.

But if you are with a person who does it God's way only as long as that does not interfere with his or her desires, then you are with a self-ruled person, and you will always lose. To the extent that any person lives to please himself and not God, others around him lose in the long run, because when push comes to shove, that person's will reigns supreme.

So, in this passage we see a litmus test for who rules one's life: that person or God. If you are with a person who says that he or she is spiritual, and yet when spirituality runs into conflict with his or her desires and the desires win, you are with a person who puts God into a category called "self-made." They are not worshiping him as he is, but as they want him to be. They are recreating God into their own image. They are not adapting to him but having him adapt to them. All of these are signs of the "I will submit to God as long as I agree with him" club. And that is no submission at all.

So, as the passage says, if someone rejects this teaching, and reworks it to fit their desires, then they are rejecting God. He wants to be accepted as he really is, rules and all. He wants to be trusted for what he says. And when someone rewrites his values, they are not accepting who he really is.

You will be much safer with a person who fulfills one of the key things required of mankind: "to walk humbly with your God" (Micah 6:8). Such a person can in the long run truly be trusted to look out for your interests as well. Trust a person who trusts God. And if he or she is truly trusting God, that person will uphold God's value of sex within marriage.

Reminders of Reasons to Say No

So, lest we begin to sound like church lady, we will stop preaching. We do not want to sound like prudes, and we do not think the Bible wants you to sound or appear that way either. Sexuality is a part of God's good creation.

But, as you embrace your sexuality, do so with self-control, sanctity, high esteem, lovingly and not lustfully, sacrificially and not "wronging" someone, and in submission to God. Then, when you are dating, you will have built in some very good limits and expression of your sexual person. You will know, for example, how far is too far. You cannot act out inappropriately with these guidelines in place. They are appropriately confining.

And, if you say no to sex outside of marriage, you will be able to discover a few crucial things while you are dating:

1. Does he or she want you for you, or just sex?
2. Is he or she capable of the other aspects of relating and intimacy, or has this person avoided developing those by just having sex? In other words, are you with an addict?

3. Is the person carrying around a lot of baggage inside that has never been healed?
4. Can this person delay gratification as we mentioned above?
5. And, most importantly, does the person have the ability to submit to God?

We beg you. Please find out these things before you allow someone into your heart. We can promise you that you do not want to have someone residing in your heart long-term who does not love you, cannot relate to you on a soul level, has a lot of unresolved baggage, cannot delay gratification, and ignores God. *And it is difficult to keep someone out of your heart who has invaded your body.* Living according to lust, or allowing yourself to be used as the object of lust, is a sign that a lot of things are wrong. Get those things right, and dating can lead to some good places.

The Boundary of Forgiveness

Angie was twenty-four and disillusioned about sex in relationships. Having slept with more guys than she even wanted to think about, she had a "what's the use" feeling. And it started, she said, when she was fifteen. As she put it, "Once I had made a mistake, I thought that I had already blown it. I had not saved myself for that one person whom I would give my life to. So, with the next boyfriend, and the ones after him, I thought, *What's the difference? I already blew it.*"

That was before she understood the way that God looks at our failures. He does not look at us like a piece of porcelain that, once broken, is always broken. He looks at us all as broken people whom he makes new again. With his forgiveness, you can start all over and be as clean as when you began.

As the psalmist puts it, "As far as the east is from the west, so far has he removed our transgressions from us" (Psalm 103:12). Or as Hebrews puts it, "Their sins and lawless acts I will remember no more" (Hebrews 10:17). And even further, "Let us draw near to God with a sincere heart in full assurance of faith, having our hearts sprinkled to cleanse us from a guilty conscience and having our bodies washed with pure water" (Hebrews 10:22).

If you ask God to forgive you through Jesus, he sees you as a completely new person. You are clean, washed with pure water, and whatever you might have done is forgotten and put away as the east is from the west. And as Paul says, "there is no condemnation" for those who have asked for the forgiveness that Jesus gives (Romans 8:1).

So, as Angie learned, your past failure does not have to doom you to further sexual brokenness. Just because you have fallen in the past does not mean that you have ruined yourself and cannot start over. You can become clean again. You can become pure again. And as you do, you can commit to remaining pure and enjoying all of the benefits of that state.

You can develop the inner life and your ability to love. You can know if someone really loves you. You can learn how to delay gratification and give to others. You can have your underlying splits, needs, hurts, and needs healed and fulfilled so that you will not have unsatisfying relationships. And you can finally give up being God and allow him to be God for you.

If you know you are forgiven, that clean slate is a powerful boundary. You can stand upon that solid ground. You don't have to worry about the cracks in your armor because of feeling dirty from the past, or a "what's the use now" feeling. You have a new state of cleanness to protect, and dating can now be about building

deeper things than a one-night experience. It can be a place of
growth instead of brokenness.

So, ask him for that forgiveness now. If you do not know Jesus,
ask him to be your Lord. Turn to him in faith and he will cleanse
you. And then walk in that state of being guilt-free. It is a strong
state indeed. And if you do, then you can wait on the real thing.

Take-Away Tips

- You need a boundary against sex outside of marriage.
  God gives you this boundary to protect you, and it will,
  in a number of ways.
- Sex has a very high purpose, great value, dignity, and
  esteem. Do not treat it or your sexuality lightly, failing to
  give it the place it deserves.
- Sex is the highest way of expressing romantic love for a
  person; therefore it must be reserved for the highest
  romantic relationship you will have—the one with your
  spouse.
- Keeping your sexual boundaries will let you know of the
  other person's self-control, delay of gratification, ability
  to love sacrificially, and willingness to submit to God.
- Do not act out of lust. It prevents love, integration, and
  healing. And, it guarantees relational problems.
- No matter what your partner says, saying no to sex will
  be the only way you find out what he or she is like when
  he or she has to respect a limit.
- God's forgiveness is available to anyone, no matter what
  you have done. It will allow you to have a clean slate and
  start over with good sexual boundaries.

──── *Chapter 18* ────

Set Up a
Detention Hall

I love music, lots of types. But I confess that there is one type of music that I really can't stand. It is a kind of love song where someone is in love with someone who is not treating her right. That part isn't the problem. It's the mistreated person's position in the relationship, and how she is responding to the mistreater. She passively complains, whines, and hopes things will get better, with statements like:

- I'll wait forever (while you look for someone better).
- Time will heal things (while you never make a commitment for years).
- Please come back (simply because I ask you).
- Why do you treat me so? (because you can).
- I'll make you love me (even though you aren't capable of loving anyone but yourself).

There is no mistaking the love, pain, and protest of these songs, and we can all identify with the struggle of caring for someone and yet having to experience the injuries that come when they sin against us. But the solutions that these sorts of songs seem to convey do nothing to solve that pain. In fact, they are the worst possible solution.

Solving problems of love, respect, responsibility, and commitment in dating relationships is the theme of this chapter. Though no one has the power to fix anyone else, you do have the power to respond in healthy ways to your date when problems arise. And those type of healthy responses, which often involve the careful, caring use of boundaries, can go a long way toward a better relationship.

In this chapter, we will go over the principles of dealing with a dating relationship in which there are boundary violations going on. One person is losing freedom and love, and one person is "playing and not paying." It is probably obvious that the boundary buster will not be the person we address, but the "boundary bustee," the person who has lost freedom and love. This is because in a dating relationship, the one who is reaping what someone else is sowing is typically the person who is most motivated to feel the pain and do something about the problem.

Some Conflict Is Normal

When you encounter problems in your relationship, don't freak out or throw in the towel. Conflicts do not necessarily mean the end of the relationship. Problems, including boundary conflicts, are a normal part of relationships. In relationship, two people love, comfort, have fun, grow—and have conflict. As the saying goes, "What do you call two people who have conflict with each other? A relationship." That is why one of the most profound relational passages in the Bible teaches us to love, tell the truth to, and forgive each other (Ephesians 4:25–32). God has already factored in the reality of conflicts and problems in relationships. He has also, in this passage, told us how to deal with them. That is part of being connected to another person who is free, has a mind of his own, and is also a sinner.

So many people naively think they will meet a kindred spirit who will never have an argument with them—only gentle disagreements that will work out easily in a spirit of mutuality. And they are devastated or lose hope when they find themselves having long-term conflicts over responsibility, control, and freedom. People who love each other still argue over time, money, jobs, respect, and differences of opinion. This is not a sign that you have a bad dating relationship. It may be a sign, however, that you are not handling the problems in the best way. So don't give up hope on dating or on your significant other. First, give up the demand that your relationship be conflict-free, get over it, and go to the next step.

Require Boundaries in Your Relationship

Next, deal with the issue that we have mentioned before in this book: never setting a limit until there is a huge problem or crisis in your love life. Boundaries are not like a fire alarm box with the notice "break glass only in emergency." You don't wait until your back is against the wall to say you don't like what is going on. Boundaries should be woven into the fabric of your life and relationship, as something that you do and say daily. After all, setting limits is simply about being honest about what you allow and don't allow. Become a person of truth, ownership, and honesty.

More than that, ensure that boundaries are part of your dating relationship. Does your date know how you feel about how he treats you? Or do you minimize it, make excuses for it, or simply give him the silent treatment, hoping he will get the message? This is not an honest approach. It is covert and deceptive to you and to him. And this is the reason that many people encounter major boundary struggles later in their dating relationship: they weren't clear in what was okay and what was not okay with them from the beginning of the connection.

So, even though you may have a big problem in your love life today, begin to look at the big picture. Don't think that the crisis is the problem. It is more likely a symptom of character problems in either or both of you that have gone denied, unattended, or ignored. And from today on, make honesty, responsibility, respect, and freedom a required part of all aspects of your relationship: socially, emotionally, sexually, spiritually, and in every other area.

See Boundaries as Preserving the Relationship, Not Ending It

Deal with your fear of setting limits. Many people are afraid that when they begin saying no and establishing boundaries and consequences, that is a sign the relationship is over. Actually, boundaries help diagnose the character of your date and of the relationship. If you are in a relationship that ends when you disagree, it is not a healthy relationship. Someone must live a lie to maintain that kind of date. Think about the future. How can a man who refuses to listen to his wife's truth ever truly give himself up for her as Christ did for the church? (Ephesians 5:25). If your date can't hear the word *no*, the boundary is not the problem. His character is the problem.

Boundaries actually cure problems of irresponsibility, domination, and manipulation. When someone who is out of control encounters a person who cannot be controlled, he is then faced with the reality of his own consequences and frailties. Though he may not like the limits, if he has a good heart, he will submit to the limits and begin to grow up in his own boundaries. So don't get into the mind-set that boundaries are your good-bye scene. They are your introduction to preserving and repairing the love you want to have with this person.

Mark and Susan had been dating for over a year, and were getting serious. Susan had people-pleasing tendencies, so when she was unhappy that Mark was sometimes sloppy when he visited her home, she was afraid to tell him it bugged her. She thought, as compliant people do, that he would either be hurt, angry, or go away. Finally, she brought his sloppiness up to him. To her surprise, Mark appreciated her words and began to work on tidying up more. He was a good guy and didn't want to bother her with his habits. Susan learned that boundaries enriched their connection, rather than ending it. Today they are happily married, and he regularly picks up his socks.

Boundary Problem Versus Character Problem

There are so many boundary problems a dating relationship can have. Let us list a few of the possibilities:

- A guy doesn't respect his girlfriend's feelings.
- A woman blames her boyfriend whenever they have a problem.
- Someone is chronically late to scheduled events.
- A man wants to borrow money from his girlfriend.
- A woman displaces her anger at her boss onto her boyfriend.
- A man pushes a woman to be sexual with him.
- A woman is dating around behind her boyfriend's back.
- A man makes promises of commitment but doesn't back them up.
- A woman is so tied into her family that she can't invest in the relationship.
- A man becomes angry and threatens violence.
- A woman has a secret drug or alcohol problem.

Whatever problem you are dealing with, the essence of it is probably that someone is sowing a problem and not reaping the effects (the boundary buster), and someone else is reaping what he never sowed (the boundary bustee) (Galatians 6:7). That is the nature of a boundary problem in a relationship. The solution is to restructure things so the sower is also the reaper.

However, there is a deeper problem: the character of the person who is crossing the boundary. Like a well that puts out contaminated water, a person who continually violates the principles of respect, responsibility, and freedom will continue crossing boundary after boundary. Don't think that because you solved the present crisis that the issues are over. Until the character issues driving the boundary problem are dealt with, you will likely see many sorts of similar problems in that person. A person who is controlling or irresponsible will be that way in many areas of life until she has submitted her character to God's process of growth. Therefore you need to see two problems: the boundary violation, and the character of the person you are dating. They cannot be isolated from each other.

There is another aspect to character, and that is the person's heart. Some boundary busters do so because they have never had good self-control, structure, and responsibility given to them. Like an out-of-control Labrador retriever (which I have much experience with), she is a nice, caring person who inadvertently knocks over the china in the living room of your life. She isn't mean, controlling, or irresponsible. She simply doesn't have much structure. This type of person often willingly listens to your feelings about the money, time, or behavior problem. She will feel bad that her behavior hurts you and will sincerely start changing. She is a good bet for the future.

The second type of boundary buster is more resistant to boundaries. For some reason or another, he has arranged his life in such a way that he can avoid ever hearing the word *no* from anyone. He may have some of the following traits:

- Not owning his hurtfulness to you
- Blaming you for the problem
- Promising change, but never changing
- Being deceptive about the problem

- Not wanting to change because it is not convenient to him
- Having trouble delaying his own gratification
- A self-centered point of view, with little ability to see your opinion

If these are in the equation, the problem is more difficult, though it can still be solved. Bear in mind, however, that you may be dealing with a person who may change only because of the pain he experiences in consequences, not because of his desire to grow or because of his love for you. Yet remember that all of us have this sort of self-centeredness, cherishing ourselves above others and wishing we were God. Have some patience and see what God does as you set the limits.

Love, Respect, and Mutuality

As you think about approaching your date with the problem, adopt a stance of love, respect, and mutuality. Let him know that you are not punishing him or getting revenge over past hurts. Your motive is love and reconciliation. You want to solve the problem because it is getting in the way of love's growth between you two. Remember that *the reality that you are even going to the trouble of dealing with the problem shows that he is important to you.* This is the world of dating, where you can abruptly break off a relationship, no harm, no foul. Let him know that you are bringing up the problem because you care.

Show respect for his choices and feelings, too. Though he is responsible for his part of the problem, remember that he has a past, his own pain, and his own baggage. Don't get into the trap of judging and controlling him as a solution for feeling controlled yourself. I had a friend who was in a controlling relationship with a guy. Finally, she told him, "It's going to be my way this time." Controlling someone else is never the solution. The answer is "Our way this time."

Approach him also from a stance of mutuality. You are not his parent, nor God, nor someone who is without sin or weakness. As the saying goes, "The ground is all level at the Cross." Confess whatever part you have played in the problem, own it, and get into the process of changing your own character. This keeps him from being in a childlike one-down position, and keeps you out of the dangerous ground of condemning others. Many times, the one who has been transgressed against needs to apologize to the boundary violator for her own contributions, such as:

- Not speaking up when she should have
- Excusing, minimizing, or rationalizing his behavior
- Telling others her complaint without telling him
- Withdrawing or becoming passive as a form of protest
- Nagging and berating instead of problem-solving
- Threatening consequences and then not following up with them

These in no way excuse the behavior, but they do allow both parties to own their fair share of the abuse.

Draw the Line

Your best approach is to be very specific about the boundary problem with your date. Have specific events that you can draw from, what you felt when they happened, what was the problem with what happened, and what you wished had happened instead. If your date is a growing person, she will benefit from the information and want to know more, so that she won't hurt you again. If your date is resistant, the specifics will help nail down the issue in reality so that she has less room to rationalize, blame, or deny.

It is important to be very specific about where the boundary violation occurred, or where the line was crossed. Many boundary busters don't know when they cross the line of respect.

They need that information. It is unkind and unfair to leave a relationship without giving the person the courtesy of at least knowing what they are doing. Think how you would feel to have someone blow you off for no reason, leaving you hurt and in the dark. Provide the mercy that you would like (James 2:12–13).

For example, you may want to say, "Jim, I appreciate your sense of humor. It's one of the things I like about you. I don't even mind when I'm part of the joke sometimes. But when I have told you what embarrasses me and you still make fun of me in public, I get really hurt. You know I'm sensitive about my weight, I've told you. And last week at the party, you made that sarcastic comment about my diets in front of everybody. It hurt, embarrassed, and angered me. And I won't put up with you doing it again."

Jim has been warned about the boundaries. He can be funny. He can even make jokes about his girlfriend in areas where she isn't sensitive. But weight jokes are off limits! Now Jim knows when he is crossing the line.

Drawing the line may not be as easy as it looks. It requires that you define what you will and will not tolerate. Many times, people will make vague, global demands on another person and place the burden on their date to figure out what that meant. They may say, "Jim, you'd better get your act together." *What is she talking about?* Jim might rightfully think.

Drawing the line is also about dealing with the character issue underneath the violation. You don't want to end up marrying a dry sadistic comic, so to speak. Talk to your date about what you have seen behind the transgression. Does he have any awareness of this? Are you the first person on the planet who has ever said anything about this to him? For example, "It seems hostile and hurtful to me sometimes, like there is anger underneath the joke at my expense. And in our relationship, it seems that you aren't very direct when you are unhappy with me. I won't hear anything about a problem from you at all, then I get blindsided in public with a joke. I would like you to look at your tendency to do that, because it really distances me." You are not Jim's counselor, but you love him and are an important source of God's reality for his growth and maturity. Take advantage of your position for both of you.

Boundaries Are Not Consequences!

It would be a wonderful world if all you had to do would be to set a limit with your date. You would say, "Ouch. That hurts. Stop it." She would say, "Okay. Sorry." She would know what bad things to avoid, and what good things to do, and so would you. The business of developing and spreading love would continue apace. Sadly, in this fallen world, that is not the case. Information itself is a necessary but insufficient condition for most boundary-violating problems in dating.

If you are a parent, or have been around kids for a while, you realize that setting a limit is only the first step. The child still has freedom to challenge, violate, and break your rules. That freedom is necessary so that you aren't controlling her, and so that she can take full advantage of the experience of consequences that you establish when she crosses the line. That is where the real growth occurs, and where the sower begins reaping. In parenting, Mom tells her son to do his homework or he will have a consequence. He is free to neglect his homework, and does so. Then Mom calmly cancels his baseball practice for that week, and he reaps what he has sown.

Stating your boundary is not enough. You will also have to lay down a consequence and stick to it. Never make the mistake of thinking that because you have said you won't put up with something, it will never happen again. You have only told some truth about your heart. For some dates, that is enough. For many, it is simply nagging, and they will ignore it.

That is what consequences are about. Consequences are the realities you set up for when the boundary is crossed again. They involve some sort of pain for your date, so that she is faced with a learning experience or loss that helps her develop self-control, respect, and empathy for others. Consequences are God's school of discipline, and "No discipline seems pleasant at the time, but painful. Later on, however, it produces a harvest of righteousness and peace for those who have been trained by it" (Hebrews 12:11).

Remember that if this boundary problem you are having with your date is not an isolated event, it is probably a character pattern. And if that is the case, she does this habitually with other people and in other contexts. For example, if she flirts on you, she probably did it with a lot of previous boyfriends. In all likelihood, flirting is almost automatic with her. So don't expect your request, protest, or warning to be enough.

I knew a man who fell in love with a woman who wanted to stay in close contact with old boyfriends. Though he wanted to be reasonable with her needs for friendships, he felt the relationship wasn't truly exclusive, that she was not letting go of them, even though she said she was. Finally, he had to stop seeing her completely for a time until she saw that she was losing him and would be left with all the guys that love hadn't worked out with. But it took that consequence for her to change. Warnings rarely work without consequences to back them up.

What Is a Fitting Consequence?

You will need to determine what an appropriate consequence is for the infractions that keep occurring. The punishment needs to fit the crime, and each situation is different. Here are some principles to apply that provide a way of thinking about what is appropriate.

Be Motivated by Love and Truth, Not Revenge

Think of your consequences as protecting you and giving her a chance to change. They are not about making anyone change, nor are they about showing her how she made you feel when she hurt you. Leave revenge to the only One who has the right to it (Romans 12:19). In addition, the motives of love and truth will keep you out of the parent-child dynamic.

Avoid the Ultimate Consequence

It is common for people who are dating to continually resort to the Ultimate Consequence: breaking off the relationship. Breaking up with your date is not like a divorce, and it is certainly an option for some bad patterns. However, when you chronically threaten to leave someone, and that is your only consequence, the threat can lose its power. The other person can easily begin thinking, *Whatever I do wrong, you'll leave me. I will give up.* It's the same idea behind the law: you are condemned for disobeying anything and everything, so you feel disheartened and wrathful (Romans 4:15).

Breaking up is not truly a consequence, even though it is sometimes necessary. This is because it ends a relationship, rather than cures the relationship. Reserve the threat of breaking up for severe problems, such as deception, unfaithfulness, violence, spiritual conflicts, sexual infractions, and legal problems.

Think Empathically

Put yourself in your date's shoes. Think how you would feel with various consequences. Come up with a combination of compassion and severity that feels fair. It is easy to judge someone's bad activities until we are caught in a transgression ourselves.

Use Reality as Your Guide

Make the consequence fit, as much as possible, with natural consequences. Get yourself out of the way as much as you can, so your date doesn't see you as the problem, but sees his relationship with reality as the problem. A less severe problem should have a less severe consequence. Set consequences prayerfully with the help of wise friends' advice. Here are a few suggestions:

- Emotional distance: limiting the depth of emotional access you can be vulnerable with
- Physical distance: leaving the room or an event if the problem occurs again. Take separate cars to events in case you need yours.
- Time: limiting the time you spend together until the problem is resolved
- Third parties: requiring someone to help, such as a friend, pastor, or counselor
- Progression of commitment: stopping or decreasing the commitment level
- Giving up exclusivity: seeing other people until the problem is resolved

Keep in mind the function of a consequence: to protect you, and to help your date face the realities of his destructive pattern.

Points to Remember in Boundary Setting

If you care about your date, you will likely have conflicted feelings about what you are doing. Essentially, you are allowing pain to touch someone important to you. The conflict of wanting closeness, yet having to have a righteous stance with a boundaryless person, can take its toll on you. Here are a few things to make sure you have in place as you go through the process.

Stay Connected

By its very nature, truth-telling divides and separates people. It causes distance and anger between them. You may even have doubts as to whether you are doing the right thing, or can withstand the pain of keeping the limits. This is to be expected, and should show you that you cannot set limits from an isolated position. None of us possess the fortitude to alienate and be in conflict with people we love, without taking in love, support, encouragement, and feedback from those who care about us. Be sure you are plugged in to good people who will stand by you when the conflicts arise.

Avoid Reactive Friends

Use experienced, spiritually mature people for support. Avoid those who idealize you as the innocent victim and see him as nothing but a creep. These sorts of friends can bolster your confidence, but do little to help you be objective and neutral. They tend to divide relationships and can often instill a sense of entitled arrogance in others which can emotionally disqualify anyone for a relationship of mutuality. At the same time, avoid people who are critical and judgmental of you, reactively blaming all the relationship problems on you. Find people who are "for" both of you, and can see both sides of the issue. Our book *Safe People* is a good source for finding the sorts of people you need during this period.

Expect Negative Reactions

If your date has character issues that cause him to resist your limits, he may see you, rather than himself, as the problem. This may mean that he may not thank you for your honesty, but rather resent you, or worse. Do not be surprised by an angry or defensive reaction. It is helpful to remember that your date may have lived his entire life running from the reality that he is selfish, controlling, or irresponsible. And here you are putting the mirror of truth in front of him. He may shoot the messenger. This may be the tantrum he has never had, as he finally must face what he is and does, and choose to either repent or rebel against God and reality. Keep yourself protected from any angry or dangerous outbursts. Let him be angry with you, but demand respect. Don't put up with abusive or disrespectful outbursts.

Empathize with the Struggle

It is no sin to love an immature person, nor to have compassion on him. As you would do with a child, empathize with him that what you are requiring is difficult. But that doesn't mean it's not required. You might say, "Margaret, I know that it will be hard for us to be apart more until you can deal with the angry outbursts that hurt me. I will miss you. But I will wait to hear from you that you are working on these issues. Please call me when you decide."

Be Patient

Allow time for God's process to take hold. Few of us accomplish one-trial learning. Generally, it takes a few slipups, some pain, and some support to work. Don't give up on someone who is resistant, failing, or denying at first. At the same time, your date's attitude toward the process is highly revealing. If he shows no signs of submitting to God's realities, no ownership, and no attempts to change, then your patience may bear fruit in letting you know that you do not have a viable relationship. Patience has an end. It does not wait forever without a good reason.

Question His Motives

If he is responding to your boundaries, that is a good thing. But make sure of why he is. It is important that he be changing because of his relationship with God, because it is the right thing to do, and because he doesn't want to hurt you. It is less important that he be changing because he thinks that is what it will take to get you back. There are so many sad stories of abused wives who let their husbands return prematurely because the husbands manipulated them into taking them back, without making true heart changes.

Provide a Way Back to Normality

Let your date know that the consequences are not permanent (unless they are permanent fixtures having to do with self-protection, respect, and the like). Let him know exactly what has to happen for you to be close, available, and emotionally accessible to him, which is also your heart's desire, once he changes. And if he does show that he is moving and changing, truly welcome him with the trust and love that he has earned, while keeping an eye on the process. But stay out of the parental role—be his equal!

Should You Require the Growth Process?

This is an important issue. If you have boundary struggles with someone you are involved with, it makes sense to set up consequences aimed at dealing with the problem. But should you go further and require that your date enter some sort of process of spiritual or emotional growth, also? Or is this going too far, or playing moral policeman?

Let's use the example of Brent and Tina. They had been dating over a year and were in love. They had similar personal and spiritual values, and basically wanted the same things in life. They enjoyed being with each other a great deal. As they had been an exclusive item for some time, Tina felt it was reasonable to want to discuss marriage with Brent. When she did, things changed for him. He became defensive, anxious, and avoided the topic. He would say to her, "It's so perfect for us. Why can't we keep things as they are?" She didn't know what that meant. But she found, over the next few weeks, that as she pursued the question, Brent had no intentions of moving toward marriage. She was in such a bind: they seemed so right for each other, but she didn't want to date him forever.

After much prayer and counsel, Tina set some limits with Brent. She told him she would be limiting their connection and seeing other people if he was unable to make any sort of movement toward the prospect of marriage. Brent was very upset at first, but after awhile, he realized Tina had a good point. Finally, after more time, Brent also agreed to begin exploring marriage with her.

Here is the question: Tina's limit has freed her to be truthful, and it has also influenced Brent to begin moving toward marriage with her. Should she be satisfied with these results, or should she also require the process of spiritual growth for him?

In our opinion, Tina *should* look for spiritual growth from Brent—for several good reasons.

Spiritual Growth Is Not Optional

First, we believe that *everyone* needs to be involved in the process of spiritual growth. This means being in a process in which the person brings his struggles, weaknesses, and vulnerabilities to God and some safe people on an ongoing basis. This might be with a support group, Bible study, counselor, or pastor. As he confesses his sins and failings, he gets forgiveness, comfort, and truth to work through his issues over time, and God grows him up (Ephesians 4:16). In other words, the question of whether you should require a boundary-busting date to be into the process is a moot one: we all should. Would you want to risk living the rest of your life with someone who is essentially disconnected from his own soul and from God? If he does not hunger and thirst for God, growth, and change above all else, you risk a lot of emptiness and misery.

Character Growth Cures Problems

Second, if your date's boundary violation is a pattern, as opposed to a one-time specific event, it is likely tied to a character problem. He may be struggling in areas such as trust, attachment, honesty, truthfulness, or perfectionism. Whatever the issue, realize that the boundary problem is probably a symptom of a deeper issue. It is best not to be satisfied if he simply stops doing the bad thing, or starts doing the good thing. The problem functions as a signal that something needs to be addressed and healed. If you ignore it, there could be other painful signals.

Ask anyone in Alcoholics Anonymous about dry drunks. They are alcoholics who have stopped drinking without any growth process, but they are still drunks. So they see life as a drunk sees life. Their character deficits have not been touched or repaired. Go for God's true process of growth, and require spiritual growth as well.

Use Limits to Test the Relationship

Finally, there is a very practical reason for the Tinas of the world to insist that their lovable but boundary-busting Brents get into a process of spiritual growth—to test whether they really should stay together. Dating preserves the freedom of each person to leave the relationship without the fallout and damage of divorce. If Brent does not want to grow spiritually, he and Tina can part ways without their lives being legally, financially, and emotionally turned upside down. Once married, however, Tina will have a hard time requiring Brent to seek God. She is bound to him in a way that God does not want torn asunder. So it is a good thing to use the unique context of dating—being a temporary situation—to set your limits, then analyze the results.

Because your spiritual health and growth as an individual and as a couple are so important to your relationship, and because God himself requires that we grow spiritually, we believe that boundaries in this area are absolutely necessary. Find someone who loves God and who you can grow with. Then enjoy the journey together!

It is our sincere hope that you now know how to approach your date and the boundary problems you may be facing. Remember that God cares deeply for both of you, and has solutions for whatever issues you may face.

Take-Away Tips

- If you're involved with a boundary-buster, get started *today* on solving the problem.
- Don't use boundaries to end the relationship (unless you are in some sort of danger); use them to save the relationship.
- Diagnose if the boundary-buster is simply clueless or has a real character problem and difficulty with responsibility and the word *no*.
- Get feedback from safe people about the problems you are having to make sure it is a real issue.
- Be clear about what hurts or bothers you and request specific change.
- Take ownership of your part of the problem.
- State the consequences of your date's ignoring your boundary, and follow through.
- Stay integrated morally and don't get caught in the saint/sinner split. Remember that you're both good and bad.
- Insist that both of you be deeply involved in the spiritual growth process.
- See what happens after you set limits: does your date humbly repent, or become angry and blaming?

Conclusion

*A*s we were writing this book, I (Dr. Townsend) found myself reflecting on my own dating experiences and relationships. I am very grateful for those years. There are several dating relationships during that period that enriched my life and helped me grow closer to God and grow in my own character. Some people have remained friends. And hopefully they better prepared me to be a husband in my own marriage.

We hope you haven't become discouraged as you have read this book. Learning to have good boundaries in dating is work, and takes some time. However, we believe that this process pays off in benefits for many areas of your life. Hopefully, it will help you understand how to better conduct your dating life to develop love, freedom, and responsibility in both you and whoever you are dating.

And that is the view we would like for you to take away from this book. Boundaries in dating is about becoming a truthful, caring, responsible, and free person who also encourages growth in those she is in contact with. There are several aspects to always be monitoring as you date, to make sure that the good things God has designed in this process are actually occurring. We have listed six critical measures of a good dating relationship below.

Is Dating Growing Me Up?

Your dating life should be a powerful change agent for you. You are making a connection with someone, learning how to safely open up, take risks, and make decisions with him. You need to be learning about your own issues, how they affect others, and what to do about them. This helps us grow.

For example, Diane, a friend of mine, tended to give her freedom and self-control to others, being a compliant and peace-keeping type of person. This issue came up in all areas of her life, and especially in the dating arena. She would allow other's problems to become her own. Finally, a couple of guys she had gone out with spoke to her about the problem. One said, "You make it too easy for me to be selfish. You never say anything when I do something that you don't like." Diane was struck by the statement, and began working on being more honest about what she disagreed with. In time, her truthfulness matured, and her dating life also became more satisfying.

Is Dating Bringing Me Closer to God?

Your dating relationship and habits involve all parts of you: your heart, mind, and soul. God intended you to be wholly integrated in your relationships. In fact, if your spiritual parts aren't involved in dating, there is a problem. Find out if your spiritual life is deeper and more meaningful as a result of who and how you date. If you are taking all the spiritual initiative, for example, something is wrong. If you do not have the fundamentals of your faith in common, something is wrong. But if your date can challenge, encourage, and draw you closer to God through her walk with him, good things can be going on.

Am I More Able to Have Good Relationships?

In other words, evaluate your relational life. You will most likely spend many, many hours dating people. Hopefully, a result of this time is that you are able to find more satisfaction in how you relate to people. This occurs in several aspects of relationships.

- Your ability to deepen your capacity for healthy intimacy with others
- Your ability to trust and depend on others to care for your emotional needs

- Your capacity to be both loving and truthful, both with dating and nondating relationships
- Your ability to find enjoyment and fulfillment in dating
- Your ability to encourage growth in others
- Your ability to begin and end a relationship in the kindest and most honest way

If your dating life is making you withdraw, become disheartened, or choose worse people, do some investigating. Something needs to change and perhaps be repaired.

Am I Picking Better Dates Over Time?

One measurable benefit of good boundaries in dating is that you are fine-tuning the types of people you are becoming involved with. As you know yourself and people better, you should be finding those who fit who you are and want to be in closer and closer ways. In addition, you should be finding people with more mature characters, also.

Conversely, if you find that you pendulum swing, there is a problem. For example, some people get stuck in being the "parent" for one person, then go for a controlling person who becomes the parent for them. That is not progress; it is a reaction.

Am I a Better Potential Mate?

A large focus of the entire dating process needs to be on your own "marriageability." Hopefully, who and how you are dating is helping to mold you into a decent human being. If you marry, your spouse should feel like he won the lottery.

Get rid of the idea that you're fine and simply need to find the "right person." Get information in your dating life on how you might make a mate miserable. Are you selfish? Irresponsible? Detached? Inaccessible? Work on those things that disqualify you from loving a mate deeply. Often when a person begins working on his own growth, the "right person" seems to come along. Maybe God has preserved that person from your immaturity until you wouldn't wreak havoc with her!

Am I Enjoying the Ride?

Finally, even though it is important growth work, dating should be fun. You need to be having enjoyable and new experiences with the person you are getting to know. You can have great times with good people as you work on good boundaries in dating. If the bad times are more frequent than the good times, detach somewhat and evaluate what is going on. You may find that you or she needs to change something. Or you may find that the lack of enjoyment simply means you aren't the right couple. Better to find this out now than in a marriage. Dating well now can help ensure a loving, satisfying, and full marriage relationship when God brings you together in that bond.

We pray the Father's hand on all your dating relationships and activities. God bless you in your own boundaries and dating.

HENRY CLOUD, PH.D.
JOHN TOWNSEND, PH.D.
Newport Beach, California
2000

Embark on a Life-Changing Journey of Personal and Spiritual Growth

Dr. Henry Cloud   Dr. John Townsend

Dr. Henry Cloud and Dr. John Townsend have been bringing hope and healing to millions for over two decades. They have helped people everywhere discover solutions to life's most difficult personal and relational challenges. Their material provides solid, practical answers and offers guidance in the areas of *parenting, singles issues, personal growth,* and *leadership.*

Bring either Dr. Cloud or Dr. Townsend to your church or organization.

They are available for:
- Seminars on a wide variety of topics
- Training for small group leaders
- Conferences
- Educational events
- Consulting with your organization

Other opportunities to experience Dr. Cloud and Dr. Townsend:
- Ultimate Leadership workshops—held in Southern California throughout the year
- Small group curriculum
- Seminars via Satellite
- Solutions Audio Club—Solutions is a weekly recorded presentation

For other resources, and for dates of seminars and workshops by Dr. Cloud and Dr. Townsend, visit: **www.cloudtownsend.com**

For other information **Call (800) 676-HOPE (4673)**

Or write to:
Cloud-Townsend Resources
18092 Sky Park South, Suite A
Irvine, CA 92614

How People Grow

What the Bible Reveals About Personal Growth

*Dr. Henry Cloud
and Dr. John Townsend,*
Authors of Boundaries

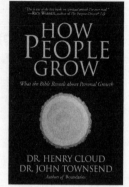

All growth is spiritual growth. Authors Drs. Cloud and Townsend unlock age-old keys to growth from Scripture to help people resolve issues of relationships, maturity, emotional problems, and overall spiritual growth. They shatter popular misconceptions about how God operates and show that growth is not about self-actualization, but about God's sanctification.

In this theological foundation to their bestselling book *Boundaries,* they discuss:

- What the essential processes are that make people grow
- How those processes fit into a biblical understanding of spiritual growth and theology
- How spiritual growth and real-life issues are one and the same
- What the responsibilities are of pastors, counselors, and others who assist people in growing—and what your own responsibilities are in your personal growth

Boundaries in Dating Workbook

Making Dating Work

Dr. Henry Cloud & Dr. John Townsend

The *Boundaries in Dating Workbook* helps readers work through the principles in the book to make the dating arena a more satisfying and productive one. It shows how taking responsibility for one's life, behavior, feelings, and values the way God intended helps develop self-control, freedom, and intimacy in the dating process. The *Boundaries in Dating Workbook* will provide readers a way to think, solve problems, and enjoy the benefits of dating in the fullest way, including increasing their abilities to find and commit to a marriage partner.

Available in stores and online!

Boundaries in Marriage

*Dr. Henry Cloud
and Dr. John Townsend*

Learn when to say yes and when to say no — to your spouse and to others — to make the most of your marriage.

Only when a husband and wife know and respect each other's needs, choices, and freedom can they give themselves freely and lovingly to one another. Boundaries are the "property lines" that define and protect husbands and wives as individuals. Once they are in place, a good marriage can become better, and a less-than-satisfying one can even be saved.

Drs. Henry Cloud and John Townsend, counselors and authors of the award-winning bestseller *Boundaries*, show couples how to apply the ten laws of boundaries that can make a real difference in relationships. They help husbands and wives understand the friction points or serious hurts and betrayals in their marriage — and move beyond them to the mutual care, respect, affirmation, and intimacy they both long for.

Boundaries in Marriage helps couples:

- Set and maintain personal boundaries and respect those of their spouse
- Establish values that form a godly structure and architecture for their marriage
- Protect their marriage from different kinds of "intruders"
- Work with a spouse who understands and values boundaries — or work with one who doesn't

Available in stores and online!

Boundaries

When to Say Yes, How to Say No, to Take Control of Your Life

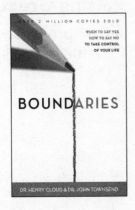

Is your life out of control?
Do people take advantage of you?
Do you have trouble saying no?
Are you disappointed with God
  because of unanswered prayers?

Having clear boundaries is essential to a healthy, balanced lifestyle. A boundary is a personal property line that marks those things for which we are responsible. In other words, boundaries define who we are and who we are not.

Boundaries impact all areas of our lives:

• Physical boundaries
• Mental boundaries
• Emotional boundaries
• Spiritual boundaries

Often, Christians focus so much on being loving and unselfish that they forget their own limits and limitations. Dr. Henry Cloud and Dr. John Townsend offer biblically based answers to many tough questions, showing us how to set healthy boundaries with our parents, spouses, children, friends, coworkers, and even ourselves.

Available in stores and online!

Other books by Drs. Henry Cloud and John Townsend

Raising Great Kids

A Comprehensive Guide to
Parenting with Grace and Truth

Boundaries with Kids

How Healthy Choices
Grow Healthy Children

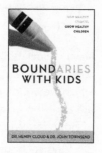

Safe People

How to Find Relationships
That Are Good for You and
Avoid Those That Aren't

The Mom Factor

Twelve "Christian" Beliefs That Can Drive You Crazy

Other books by Dr. Henry Cloud

Changes That Heal

How to Understand Your Past
to Ensure a Healthier Future

Other books by Dr. John Townsend

Hiding from Love

How to Change the Withdrawal
Patterns That Isolate and Imprison You